THE THAMES PATH

by Leigh Hatts

2 POLICE SQUARE, MILNTHORPE, CUMBRIA LA7 7PY
www.cicerone.co.uk

© Leigh Hatts 1998, 2005, 2016
Third edition 2016
ISBN: 978 1 85284 829 3
Second edition 2005
ISBN-10: 1 85284 436 1
ISBN-13: 978 1 85284 436 3
First edition 1998
ISBN: 1 85284 270 9

All photographs are by the author unless otherwise stated.
A catalogue record for this book is available from the British Library.
Printed in China on behalf of Latitude Press Ltd

© Crown copyright OS PU100012932 NASA relief data (Appendix A mapping only) courtesy of ESRI Appendix A route mapping by Lovell Johns
www.lovelljohns.com

Acknowledgements

The author is grateful for help from David Sharp, Jane Bowden, Rosemary Clarke, Stephen Green, James Hatts (for transport information), Jos Joslin, Marion Marples, Paul Newman and many others over the years.

Updates to this Guide

While every effort is made by our authors to ensure the accuracy of guidebooks as they go to print, changes can occur during the lifetime of an edition. Any updates that we know of for this guide will be on the Cicerone website (www.cicerone.co.uk/829/updates), so please check before planning your trip. We also advise that you check information about such things as transport, accommodation and shops locally. Even rights of way can be altered over time. We are always grateful for information about any discrepancies between a guidebook and the facts on the ground, sent by email to info@cicerone.co.uk or by post to Cicerone, 2 Police Square, Milnthorpe LA7 7PY, United Kingdom.

Front cover: View from Richmond Hill above Petersham (Stage 3)

CONTENTS

The Thames Path

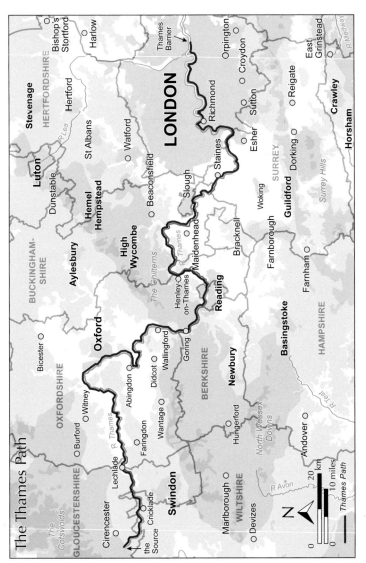

ROUTE SUMMARY TABLE

Stage	Start	Finish	Distance	Page
1	Thames Barrier	Tower Bridge	9 miles (14.5km)	15
2	Tower Bridge	Putney	10 miles (16km)	31
3	Putney	Kingston	13 miles (20.9km)	50
4	Kingston	Chertsey	11 miles (17.7km)	66
5	Chertsey	Staines	4 miles (6.4km)	78
6	Staines	Windsor	7½ miles (12km)	83
7	Windsor	Maidenhead	6½ miles (10.5km)	92
8	Maidenhead	Marlow	7 miles (11.2km)	101
9	Marlow	Henley	8½ miles (13.6km)	109
10	Henley	Reading	9 miles (14.5km)	119
11	Reading	Pangbourne	7 miles (11.2km)	128
12	Pangbourne	Goring	4 miles (6.4km)	134
13	Goring	Wallingford	7 miles (11.2km)	138
14	Wallingford	Dorchester	5 miles (8km)	146
15	Dorchester	Abingdon	9 miles (14.5km)	152
16	Abingdon	Oxford	9½ miles (15.2km)	161
17	Oxford	Newbridge	13½ miles (21.7km)	173
18	Newbridge	Lechlade	16 miles (25.7km)	182
19	Lechlade	Cricklade	10½ miles (16.8km)	194
20	Cricklade	The Source	12¼ miles (19.7km)	202

Total 180 miles (288km)

Route symbols on OS map extracts

route

alternative route/detour

start point

finish point

start/finish point

direction of walk

For OS symbols key see OS maps

Ashton Keynes (Stage 20)

INTRODUCTION

The 180-mile Thames Path from London to Gloucestershire is the only long-distance route to follow a river throughout its length from tidal waters, and also the only one to pass through London and major towns. As much as 90 per cent of the path is public footpath or bridleway. Walking the trail can easily take three weeks if you want to explore every town and village. Or you could spend years relishing the experience in a series of short weekend sections as public transport is plentiful. And then, having walked one way you may well be tempted to walk back and enjoy the equally splendid views from the other direction.

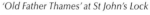

TOWPATH TO NATIONAL TRAIL

As early as the 1880s there was a suggestion that the Thames towpath, falling into disuse as traffic turned from the river to railways, should be preserved as a long-distance recreational route. In the next century the call was taken up after the First World War by the Council for the Protection of Rural England and after the Second World War by the Thames Conservancy's River Thames Walk Committee.

Thirty years later the Ramblers' Association and River Thames Society managed to persuade the Thames Water Authority and the Countryside Commission to produce a feasibility study on a continuous route from

'Old Father Thames' at St John's Lock

London to the source making use of the remaining sections of towpath. This was eventually published in 1985 and government approval for the Thames Path was given in 1989. The route was officially opened, following the creation of 16 miles of new riverside path and three bridges, in 1996.

THE PATH TODAY

Through London

The birth of a riverside path in London coincides with a realisation that the capital's waterway offers great opportunities both on and off the water. In the 1980s it looked as if the Thames might become merely a highway for barges taking London's rubbish downstream to Rainham or Mucking Marshes. However, by 1986 the Pool of London had as many as 36 cruise-liners and naval vessels passing under Tower Bridge in a year. Now piers have been built for a riverbus service.

As many as 44 different bird species have been recorded at the Thames Barrier where the national trail starts. The tidal-Thames, fishless at the start of the 20th century, is the cleanest metropolitan river in the world, with an estuary supporting 115 species of fish and playing a part in supporting North Sea fish stocks. Salmon, extinct in Greater London since 1833 due to pollution, returned in the 1980s. Smelt, a cousin of the salmon, thrive in good water and congregate below Gravesend in winter and in spring

10

come upstream in shoals to spawn at Wandsworth. Eels pass through central London in early summer. London now has an increasing number of swans, although only a few years ago they were so scarce that the annual swan count was abandoned.

Upper Reaches

Long before the Thames turns non-tidal, near the Greater London boundary, the river becomes a green corridor running out of the capital. The upper reaches are varied. The water can be a busier highway at Maidenhead and Henley than in London. Elsewhere, especially above Oxford, water and towpath can be both beautiful and lonely. Here accommodation and transport needs to be carefully planned.

In the Home Counties and even in far-off Wiltshire there are reminders of London. Duchy of Lancaster territory is encountered around the Savoy and at Kempsford; Shelley knew the Thames from London to Lechlade, and William Morris lived by the river both at Hammersmith and near the end of navigation at Kelmscott. Stone for St Paul's Cathedral came downstream from Oxfordshire.

The Source

The climax to the 180-mile walk is an empty field with an often dry spring. Fortunately there is a nearby pub with strong Thames connections and the first convenient railway station since Oxford.

Swans near Old Man's Bridge in Oxfordshire

WILDLIFE

Moorhens and voles are seen in quiet pools, although they are at risk from the increase in mink which have no natural predator in Britain. Herons and cormorants are a familiar sight around Putney and even in Docklands. Ducks are found as far downstream as Blackfriars. Deer will be encountered, and there are still many reaches where cattle are watered at the river's natural bank.

LOOKING AFTER THE RIVER

In 1197 Richard I, who was short of money after the Crusades, sold the river conservancy to the Corporation of London, which in 1857 reluctantly handed it over to the Thames Conservancy Board. In fact the City had for much of the time laid little claim to the non-tidal Thames, which by 1757 was controlled by Thames Navigation Commissioners who built the towpath. Since 1909 the 96-mile tidal Thames from Teddington to the sea has been under the control of the Port of London Authority. In 1974 Thames Conservancy, controlling the non-tidal river as far as Cricklade, was succeeded by the Thames Water Authority, which gave way in 1989 to the even more short-lived National Rivers Authority. The present Environment Agency was formed in 1995.

The Countryside Commission's Thames Path Officer is Steven Tabbitt, who also looks after the Ridgeway which crosses the Thames at Goring.

Tenfoot Bridge, between Newbridge and Lechlade

His address is The National Trails Office, Signal Court, Old Station Way, Eynsham, Oxford OX29 4TL (tel 01865 810224; thames.path@ oxfordshire.gov.uk). Flood information is available from the Environment Agency on 08459 881188 or 0345 988 1188.

ACCOMMODATION AND TRANSPORT

Each chapter includes a short accommodation list, although returning to London each day by rail is easy as far as Oxford. The Thames Path National Trail Companion, issued by the National Trails Office, has addresses for bed and breakfast, camping and hostels. Accommodation lists are also

included on the Thames Path section of the National Trail website: www. nationaltrail.co.uk.

Most of the Thames Path is easily accessible by public transport as indicated at the end of each section.

MAPS

The following nine OS Explorer maps (1:50,000) cover the entire Thames Path: 160 (Windsor), 161 (London South), 162 (Greenwich), 169 (Cirencester and Swindon), 168 (Stroud), 170 (Abingdon), 171 (Chiltern Hills West), 172 (Chiltern Hills East), 173 (London North) and 180 (Oxford). It should be noted that 171 (Chiltern Hills West) overlaps with 159 (Reading), which also shows the Thames between Shiplake and Pangbourne.

SAFETY

The Thames has many moods. In London it offers peace among the chaos, but it can also be 'the dangerous Thames', with fast currents and cold water. At low tide the beach at Hammersmith can suck a human being into the mud and you can easily be cut off by tides. London's lifeboats are called out on average twice a day and Tower Bridge lifeboat has the highest number of call-outs in the UK.

The non-tidal upper reaches also have deep waters, and the tempting Duxford ford can often be too dangerous to cross. A drought can result in a slower water flow susceptible to freezing, but still not safe to walk on.

USING THIS GUIDE

This book is a guide for those who want to walk upstream along the Thames Path from London to Gloucestershire, and is therefore an alternative to the official Countryside Agency guide designed to assist walkers heading from the river's source downstream to the capital.

It includes a possible diversion at Culham to visit the attractive village of Sutton Courtenay on the Old Thames. However, London's left-bank alternative route, designated by Natural England as an afterthought, is not included, as it is felt that long-distance walkers will prefer the original right-bank path, which avoids traffic and affords a fine view of the City of London.

This guide maintains tradition by referring to the left bank and right bank rather than the north and south bank. Banks can also be east and west. The left or right bank is the one that is on your left or right when you are looking downstream – ie back towards London.

Each stage is illustrated with extracts from the OS 1:50,000 mapping and the step-by-step route description is packed with information about local history and sights along the route. At the end of each stage, information is given about refreshment stops, accommodation, public transport and tourist information offices, where available, and the map(s) required to study the route and its environs in more detail.

Countryside Code

On rural stretches the Countryside Code should always be followed.

- Be safe – plan ahead and follow any signs.
- Leave gates and property as you find them.
- Protect plants and animals, and take your litter home.
- Keep dogs under close control.
- Consider other people.

Tower Bridge

STAGE 1
Thames Barrier to Tower Bridge

Start	Thames Barrier
Finish	Tower Bridge
Distance	9 miles (14.5km)

The first section, which can easily be a day's walk if pauses are made at the landmarks, passes along the Greenwich waterfront and through Surrey Docks into central London. There are fine views of the O2 and the Isle of Dogs, with its famous Canary Wharf Tower seen from many angles. The first view of St Paul's Cathedral in central London is at Greenwich.

The nearest station to the Thames Barrier is Charlton. Go left out of the station to a crossroads and turn right along Woolwich Road. Just beyond the second roundabout go left into Eastmoor Street. Bear right into the parkland to join the Green Chain Walk which leads to steps up to the top of the floodbank by the Barrier.

For 1:25K route map see booklet pages 82–85.

Thames Barrier and the O2

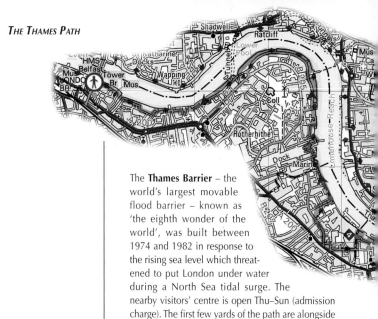

The **Thames Barrier** – the world's largest movable flood barrier – known as 'the eighth wonder of the world', was built between 1974 and 1982 in response to the rising sea level which threatened to put London under water during a North Sea tidal surge. The nearby visitors' centre is open Thu–Sun (admission charge). The first few yards of the path are alongside a river-profile map by artist Simon Read.

The 180-mile route starts at the end of the promenade immediately downstream of the Thames Barrier where there is a notice over the Thames Path entrance. Follow the covered path and beyond the flood-protection steps turn back to join a riverside path known as Nagasaki Walk.

After the Anchor and Hope the path is marked by bricks in the road. Beyond the former Cory's bargeworks on Durham Wharf the road turns inland, leaving the path to run ahead under the conveyors of a working wharf. This path rejoins the river before turning up the side of the Greenwich Yacht Club. At the back of the club go right on a rising path.

At a junction at the edge of the Millennium Village wetlands turn right to rejoin the river. Continue along the riverside to go under the Emirates Air Line and pass the O2 pier and then the O2 at Blackwell Point on the Greenwich Peninsula. The view across the water is of the lighthouse at the mouth of the River Lea.

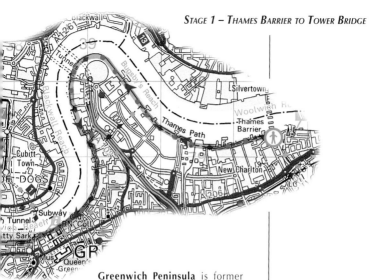

Greenwich Peninsula is former marshland. A lonely war memorial is a survivor from the gasworks which covered the area for a century from 1881. The Blackwall Tunnel road link to the north bank was opened in 1897 for horse-drawn traffic. The Millennium Dome, now the O2, has led to the area being branded North Greenwich after the new station which serves the growing Millennium Village. However, the Pilot pub opened in 1805.

Greenwich

The riverside path curves round the O2, passing Richard Wilson's Slice of Reality sculpture which gives the impression of a moored ship. As the path turns southwest the Greenwich Meridian is marked on the ground.

Once on the west side of the O2, cross the top of Drawdock Road, which runs into the river, and return to the riverside. There is a small hop field (left) belonging to Greenwich's Meantime Brewery. Stay by the river to go over Delta Wharf. At a junction keep ahead to cross Victoria Deep Water Terminal. (There may be temporary short tunnels for the path to protect walkers when gravel is being unloaded.) At the far end the path goes inland and round the back of Bay Wharf. At a T-junction go right to rejoin the river at Blackwall Reach. There is a view across the water to Millwall Reach on the Isle of Dogs.

Blackwall Reach includes working wharves. Morden Wharf is named after Sir John Morden, who founded nearby Blackheath's Morden College in 1695. On Enderby's Wharf the Enderby brothers set up a rope walk in 1834, and during Antarctic whaling expeditions discovered Enderby Land and Greenwich Island. General Gordon, a relative, spent his last night in England at Enderby House, built in 1846. Later the first successful transatlantic telegraph cable was manufactured at Enderby's Wharf. Cobbled Ballast Quay, with its mid-Victorian harbour master's office, is where ships took on Blackheath gravel as ballast for return voyages. The Cutty Sark Tavern mainly dates from 1804.

The Isle of Dogs, known as Stepney Marsh until Henry VIII had his kennels built there, was called an island even before becoming a real island in 1805 when West India Dock was given an eastern entrance. Today's landmark is the 50-storey Canary Wharf Tower.

Follow the path to Ballast Quay. (There are possible diversions for the building of a liner terminal.) Beyond

The Isle of Dogs

the Cutty Sark Tavern, the Thames Path again crosses the Meridian before passing the power station and reaching Trinity Hospital.

> **Trinity Hospital**, home to 21 local men, was founded in 1613 by Lord Northampton, whose tomb (by Nicholas Stone) is in the chapel, having been moved from Dover about 1770. The battlements were added in 1812. High tides are recorded on the river wall. The adjoining power station was built in 1906 to supply London's trams.

Keep ahead along a passage behind High Bridge Wharf, passing High Bridge Drawdock and the Yacht, to find the Trafalgar Tavern.

> **The Trafalgar Tavern**, opened in 1837, was famous for its annual whitebait dinner, when the prime minister and cabinet arrived by barge. The fish was caught locally and cooked within the hour. Charles Dickens set the wedding breakfast in *Our Mutual Friend* here, and the artist Tissot featured the river frontage in 1878 sketches and an oil painting. The next-door Curlew Rowing Club, founded in 1866, is the tideway's oldest.

Take the narrow path in front of Greenwich's Royal Naval College.

GREENWICH

The former Royal Naval College buildings, now occupied by the University of Greenwich, are on the site of a Tudor palace where Henry VIII was born and where he married Catherine of Aragon. The College's Painted Hall and chapel are open daily; admission free. Wren's buildings, intended as a naval version of Chelsea Hospital, frame the Queen's House, designed by Inigo Jones for James I's wife and built to span the line of the old main road. It is now part of the National Maritime Museum, as is the Observatory on the hill. St Alphege's stands on the site of Archbishop Alphege's martyrdom by invading Danes in 1012. Composer Thomas Tallis and General Wolfe are buried inside. The Cutty Sark tea clipper, in dry dock since 1954, provides the skyline of masts for the townscape.

The Greenwich foot tunnel is also part of the Thames Path, which from here to Teddington at the end of the tidal Thames runs along both sides. This guide follows the original route on the south side.

Pass the *Cutty Sark* and the foot tunnel entrance. After a short distance pass Horseferry Place (left) and go through covered Wood Wharf to reach New Capital Quay. Keep forward along Dreadnaught Walk to pass Costa Coffee and Waitrose in Victoria Parade (left). Dreadnaught Walk leads directly to a new swing bridge spanning the entrance to Deptford Creek.

Deptford Creek is the mouth of the River Ravensbourne, which rises in Bromley. 'Deptford' means 'deep ford'. When the *Golden Hinde* moored here in 1581 Elizabeth I went on board to knight Sir Francis Drake. Both the road and rail bridges can open to let tall ships up river. The Laban Dance Centre, designed by Tate Modern architects Herzog and de Meuron, opened in 2003.

Once on the Deptford bank go right past a statue of Peter the Great. Stay with the Thames as far as the Ahoy Centre, where the path turns inland to Deptford Green.

DEPTFORD

Deptford was a fishing village that Henry VIII turned into a naval dockyard. Trinity House, the coastal pilotage authority, started here as 'The Guild of the Most Glorious Trinity of Deptford'. St Nicholas's medieval Kentish tower was a shipping landmark. The charnel house where bodies found in the river were stored survives. Buried in the churchyard is playwright Christopher Marlowe, who was mysteriously murdered nearby in 1593. (Thomas Archer's outstanding St Paul's was built behind the High Street in 1730.) Here the Mary Rose was built, and Elizabeth I dined on the *Golden Hinde*. Diarist John Evelyn lived at Sayes Court, where in 1698 Peter the Great of Russia stayed incognito studying shipbuilding. After 1869 the dockyard was used for cattle ships and the meat trade. Convoys Wharf, used for landing newsprint until 2000, was the last working dock. The ferry steps remain at the end of Watergate Street, which is a continuation of the High Street, a rare survival of a 19th-century shopping street, with two pie-and-mash shops.

Keep forward along Borthwick Street. At the double bend go right to follow the side of Paynes Wharf. At the far end bear half left under an arch. At the end of Paynes Wharf turn inland along narrow Watergate Street. Keep ahead at a junction and go right into Prince Street to pass the Dog & Bell and Convoys Wharf entrance.

Just before the main road turn right down cobbled Sayes Court Street at the side of Chester House to enter Sayes Court Park (the site of Evelyn's house). Bear left through the garden to reach Grove Street. Turn right and later go right into Pepys Park. Take the red path which leads to a gap in the buildings ahead. Walk up the wide stairs. Go through a gap on the left to follow a path leading on to Deptford Strand.

Deptford Strand was from 1858 to 1961 the Royal Victualling Yard. The riverfront buildings are former rum warehouses. A gateway to the offices of the Porter and Clerk of Cheque survive elsewhere on the housing estate, named after Navy Secretary Samuel Pepys who had an office here in the 17th century. At the west end is 16-storey Aragon Tower, built in 1962

and containing 144 council flats, and converted by
Berkeley Homes in 2004. Across the river by the pier
is Burrell's Wharf, where Isambard Brunel's *Great
Eastern* steamship was launched in 1858.

The promenade continues across St George's Wharf
where there are the Deptford–Rotherhithe boundary stones. Go over South Dock's lock gates and right
to pass the rebuilt Dog and Duck Stairs (named after a
disappeared pub) by Greenland Pier. Continue along the
riverside to the Greenland Dock entrance crossed by a
swing bridge.

> **Greenland Dock**, named after its whaling connec-
> tions and dating from 1700, was enlarged in 1904.

Stay on the riverfront along Swedish Quays and
below King Frederick IX Tower to turn inland down
Randall Rents – not ahead on the wooden walkway.

> **Randall Rents** is named after John Randall, who
> committed suicide in 1803 by jumping from a win-
> dow of Nelson Dock House (see below). The alley,
> dating from 1698 and once called Wet Dock Lane,
> was lined with housing for workers of Randall's
> Shipyard, which around 1800 was the second larg-
> est in London.

On reaching the back of the Ship and Whale, go
right to follow Odessa Street along the back of rebuilt
New Caledonian Wharf. At the bend turn right on to
Commercial Pier Wharf and Barnard's Wharf.

> **Barnard's Wharf** housing was completed in 1992.
> As Barnard's Dockyard there was a substantial slip-
> way here.

The path leads to Surrey Docks Farm. (If gates are
locked go through estate and right to follow road round
to farm entrance and up an alley.)

Surrey Docks Farm started on the south side of Greenland Dock entrance in 1975 and moved here to South Wharf in 1986. The organic farm sells eggs, cheese, honey and goats' milk. The café is open daily except Mondays.

At the end of the farm's riverside path go right to join Trinity Wharf leading to Durand's Wharf where there are gym facilities. Continue along Swedish Quays but just before Nelson Dock go left and right to the dock.

Nelson Dock takes its name from Nelson Wake who rented the dock in the 1820s. When Nelson Dock House was built in 1740 it faced fields and was flanked by timber yards. (Logs were landed at downstream Lawrence Wharf until 1986.) Between 1687 and 1888 at least 114 ships were built here, including naval gunships. From the 1750s until 1821 Randall and Brent pioneered steam shipbuilding, and in the 1850s Bilbe and Perry pioneered

Sculpture at Surrey Docks Farm

timber cladding on iron frames for China tea clippers. The yard closed in 1968 and in 1989 the dock was renamed Port Nelson and flats built. When they failed to sell, the complex became a hotel and reverted to its original name. Upstream Columbia Wharf (part of the hotel) is a late Victorian granary.

Cross the inland end of the dock to go down steps on the left and turn right along the Rotherhithe Street. Pass the gates of Nelson House (right) and continue along the road, past the Blacksmiths Arms, and right up an alley known as Horn Stairs.

Horn Stairs, once known as Cuckold's Point, probably takes its name from the ducking stool here (on the Canada Wharf site), which had a set of horns on top of its wooden structure as late as the 1750s. Downstream Canada Wharf is a former timber warehouse. The upstream houses were built in 1994–5 on Ordnance Wharf leadworks which closed in 1982 and Sunderland Wharf.

Continue along the riverside to pass a decorative obelisk and Pageants Stairs. After a short distance cross the former Lavender Dock entrance to reach Sovereign View. Across the street to the left is the now much reduced Lavender Pond.

Sovereign View, a housing development completed in 1993, covers the former Lavender Wharf occupied until 1985 by Burmah Castrol's oil depot. In the 18th century the site had been occupied by shipwrights. Lavender Pond behind the dock entrance is a two-acre nature park formed from the remains of a vast dock of the same name. The pumphouse reopened in 1991 as the Rotherhithe Heritage Museum, displaying dockers' tools and the result of local beach combing (open occasionally 9am–4pm; free). Across the river is the entrance to Limehouse Basin and the London canal system.

At Globe Stairs the path returns to the road opposite the Pizza Lounge. Turn right on the road along the back of Globe Wharf.

Globe Wharf Rice Mill was built in 1883, and for almost a century the six-storey building handled all rice coming into London.

Turn right up the far side of Globe Wharf to walk along King and Queen Wharf which leads on to Prince's Riverside.

Prince's Riverside is the former Bellamy's Wharf aggregates depot, which closed in 1992 to be redeveloped as flats, with the riverside path running on a bridge across the dock inlet. At the far end is Bull Head Dock Wharf, once specialising in ship breaking and resale of timbers, where the *Téméraire* was broken up just after JMW Turner had painted her here.

Globe Wharf Rice Mill near Rotherhithe

25

The path leads to the Old Salt Quay pub next to Surrey Basin Entrance drawbridge.

Surrey Basin Entrance gave access to nine other major docks. The first ship entered in 1807. The Old Salt Quay pub, resembling a boathouse was built in 1995 on Dinorwic Wharf. The large YHA building behind opened in 1991.

Cross the drawbridge ahead and just beyond Octagon Court (right) go right up steps on to Clarence Wharf.

Clarence Wharf belonged to Surrey Consumers' Gas Company. The pier was built in 1860 for the landing of coal for the gasworks which closed in 1959. Sea-dredged aggregates, which were unloaded at high tide into hoppers running above the street, replaced coal until the wharf closed in 1992. The riverside path opened in 1997 shortly after Brunel Point housing development was completed. Restoration of the pier for public access was part of the planning consent.

Further on is Cumberland Wharf, which at the far end has a statue recalling the Pilgrim Fathers. Return to Rotherhithe Street, to pass a former barge builders and the Brunel tunnel house (left).

Rotherhithe Street narrows to run between warehouses including Hope Sufferance Wharf. At a junction go right to climb steps. Beyond King's Stairs the path is in an arcade with the first view of Tower Bridge. A little further on, the way is briefly blocked by the former Braithwaite and Dean's lighterage office – once part of a terrace. The Angel marks the end of Rotherhithe Street.

The Angel, dating from at least 1682, is the successor to the Salutation on the site run by nearby Bermondsey Abbey. Samuel Pepys and Captain Cook both visited. The painter James Whistler sketched Rotherhithe from the balcony, reputed to

ROTHERHITHE

Rotherhithe was a market garden village which became a shipbuilding centre. The church was rebuilt in 1715, but in the crypt is a medieval base incorporating Roman bricks. The interior pillars are ships' masts and the Epiphany Chapel altar is made from *Téméraire* wood (see above). To the left of the sanctuary is a plaque to Captain Christopher Jones of the Pilgrim Fathers' *Mayflower*, which in 1620 sailed to America from the jetty behind the Mayflower (once licensed to sell British and US stamps to visiting sailors). It opened as the Shippe in 1515, and as the Spread Eagle was used during 1825–43 by men digging Brunel's Thames Tunnel ('the Great Bore'), intended as a foot and horse crossing but converted for trains in 1865–9 (now the East London Line). The Rotherhithe road tunnel opened in 1908 after 3000 people had been moved. Although the docks closed in 1970 two Scandinavian churches remain in Albion Street. The toilets at the end of the street used to have Men and Women signs in Norwegian and English. In Rotherhithe churchyard there is the Wilson family tomb, containing the body of Prince Lee Boo of the Pelau Islands who sailed here in the 1780s with Captain Wilson. Rotherhithe is the childhood home of actor Michael Caine and entertainer Max Bygraves.

be haunted by Judge George Jeffreys who watched the executions on Wapping beach opposite. Across the road are the remains of Edward III's palace – hence nearby King's Stairs. The life-size figures of local doctor and MP Alfred Salter and his wife Ada, with daughter and cat, are by the river.

Continue past the palace remains and along Bermondsey Wall East to reach Cherry Garden Pier.

Cherry Garden Pier was used in 1664 by Samuel Pepys when visiting the pleasure garden. Later it was popular with those taking the waters at Bermondsey Spa in the 1760s. The pier was JMW Turner's vantage point for his painting *The Fighting Téméraire*, showing the Trafalgar ship arriving at sunset to be broken up.

At Fountain Green Square turn inland to rejoin Bermondsey Wall East. The way round Chambers Wharf cold store site is down Loftie Street, right into Chambers Street and right again up East Lane to a junction at East Lane Stairs.

East Lane Stairs, also known as Sterling Wharf Stairs, is a lightermen's landing point. Alongside is number 33, a former grain store built in 1866.

Go left along Bermondsey Wall West to an area known as Jacob's Island, where there is a brief view of houseboats. Ahead is the sharp turn into Mill Street.

Mill Street is one side of St Saviour's Dock. The 1885 New Concordia Wharf flour mill was one of Docklands' first conversions, being begun in 1980 when Vogan's Mill pea-splitting, pearl barley and lentil mills still operated, with Spillers dog biscuit factory opposite. Ship's biscuit manufacturer George Frean founded Peek-Frean's in 1858 in Mill House (south of Wolesey Street), where Garibaldi biscuits were first made. Jacob Street marks the centre of Jacob's Island – once a slum surrounded by stagnant water ditches fed by the diverted Neckinger stream (see St Saviour's Dock, below) and depicted in Charles Dickens' *Oliver Twist*. In 1849 the *Morning Chronicle* described this area as 'the Venice of drains' and 'the very capital of Cholera'.

The path does not go sharp left with the road into Mill Street, but ahead into New Concordia Wharf (open 7am–10pm) to bear right through a passage. Cross St Saviour's Dock to reach Tea Trade Wharf on the corner of the dock and the beginning of Butler's Wharf.

St Saviour's Dock was formed by the mouth of the now-diverted River Neckinger on which Bermondsey Abbey had a tide-mill. 'Neckinger' is said to come from 'neckcloth', with which pirates were hanged here. Shad Thames, behind Java and Cinnamon Wharves on the western side, is the best-preserved dockland canyon street, where the last working spice mill provided the original aroma until 1994. The pedestrian swingbridge, designed by architect and local resident Nicholas Lacey, was added in 1996.

Butler's Wharf is a collection of former bonded warehouses. A man who worked here in 1937 recalled: 'We had just about everything coming through ... rubber, cocoa, coffee, cassia, cardamons, canned salmon, ginger, dates, nutmeg, wines, spirits ...' After the wharf closed in 1972 the streets were used for filming *The French Lieutenant's Woman* and *Dr Who*. The main building, dating from 1875, now includes Terence Conran's Le Pont de la Tour restaurant, where Tony Blair and President Clinton once dined. At the west end is the former Courage Brewery which operated from 1789 until 1981. The view is of St Katharine Dock entrance.

Walk along Butler's Wharf promenade to pass the restaurants and pier Narrow Maggie Blake's Cause takes the path back to Shad Thames. Go right to Tower Bridge.

FACILITIES INFORMATION – THAMES BARRIER TO TOWER BRIDGE

Refreshments
Ballast Quay: Cutty Sark Tavern. 11am–11pm (Sun 12–10.30pm).
  Food 12–10pm (Sat 12–9pm).
Surrey Docks Farm: Café open daily 10am–4pm except Mon.
Surrey Docks Entrance: Old Salt Quay pub open 11am–11pm
  (Sun 10am–11pm). Food until 10pm.
Rotherhithe: The Mayflower, Rotherhithe Street. 11am–11pm
  (Sun 12–10.30pm). Bar snacks until 8pm.

Accommodation
Rotherhithe: YHA, 20 Salter Road SE16 5PR (0845 371 9756, www.yha.org.uk).

Transport
Thames Barrier: National Rail to Charlton.
Greenwich: National Rail and Docklands Light Railway.
Tower Bridge: Underground from Tower Hill.

Tourist Information
Greenwich: Cutty Sark Gardens (0870 608 2000).

Map
OS Explorer 162 (Greenwich) and 173 (London North).

STAGE 2
Tower Bridge to Putney

Start	Tower Bridge
Finish	Putney Bridge
Distance	10 miles (16km)

This section takes the path from the Pool of London through central London by way of Bankside, the South Bank, Lambeth Palace, Battersea and Wandsworth to the start of the towpath at Putney. The views are of the City of London and St Paul's Cathedral, the Palace of Westminster, Chelsea and Fulham.

Tower Bridge, completed in 1894, with the draw-bridges' weights in steel towers clothed in Gothic-style stone, was raised more than 6000 times in its first year. Now it opens about 500 times. The public is admitted to the interior daily 10am–5.15pm (4pm winter); admission charge.

For 1:25K route map see booklet pages 78–82.

From below the south end of Tower Bridge turn upstream into Potters Fields, which faces the Tower of London.

Potters Fields recalls Roman pottery found here. The park opened in 1988, embracing a burial ground (tombstones in south corner) and Pickle Herring Street, which continued westwards from under Tower Bridge behind wharves overlooking the Tower of London. City Hall, offices of the Mayor of London and the London Assembly, was designed by Norman Foster and opened in 2002. The glass buildings beyond the Scoop are the More London development, completed in 2003 and occupied by Ernst and Young and Visit London.

 The Tower Of London dates from William the Conqueror's reign. The moat, fed by the Thames, was added 200 years later and only filled in during the 19th century on the orders of the Duke of Wellington.

Continue past the permanently moored HMS *Belfast* and Southwark Crown Court to reach Hay's Wharf.

Hay's Wharf was started in 1651 by Alexander Hay, who bought the Abbot of Battle's Inn (the abbot's London house) on the site of Hay's Galleria – the 1850s inlet dock turned shopping arcade. The Horniman pub recalls the tea clippers which called here from 1862 – in 1950 a million tea chests were landed. New Zealand butter and cheese started arriving in 1867 and Hay's became 'London's larder' until closure in 1970. At the west end is the wharf office, St Olaf House, built in 1931 to Goodhart-Rendel's continental–modern design on the site of St Olave's Church. Across the water are Custom House and the former Billingsgate Fish Market.

Beyond the pier, but before London Bridge, leave the Pool of London by turning down a narrow path by St Olaf House and go right to pass under London Bridge

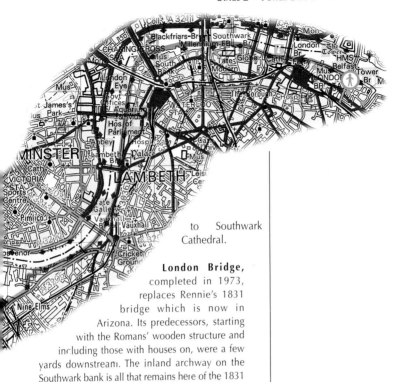

to Southwark Cathedral.

London Bridge, completed in 1973, replaces Rennie's 1831 bridge which is now in Arizona. Its predecessors, starting with the Romans' wooden structure and including those with houses on, were a few yards downstream. The inland archway on the Southwark bank is all that remains here of the 1831 bridge.

Southwark Cathedral, London's oldest Gothic church and a cathedral since 1905, was founded as a convent in 606 and became a priory in 1106. As Southwark's parish church it was known to William Shakespeare, whose brother was buried in the chancel in the same year as John Harvard of Harvard University fame was baptised here. Behind the cathedral is Borough Market.

At the cathedral's west end turn right to pass St Mary Overie Dock (home of the *Golden Hinde* replica) and enter Clink Street by the palace ruin.

St Paul's Cathedral from Bankside

Winchester Palace The roofless dining hall with its 1370 rose window is the remains of the Bishop of Winchester's residence. This was within the diocese and the bishop had a house here from 1109 until 1626. St Thomas Becket stayed a night just weeks before his murder. Catherine of Aragon slept here on her arrival in London, Henry VIII visited, and Mary I and her new husband Philip of Spain dined here before entering the City opposite. Clink Street recalls the 'Clink' prison beneath the palace kitchen now occupied by Pret A Manger. The palace parkland ran west as far as Tate Modern.

Continue ahead to pass the Clink Museum and go under Cannon Street railway bridge. Turn right to rejoin the river at the Anchor.

The Anchor was a pub on the bishop's estate in Shakespeare's time. Samuel Pepys came to watch the Great Fire of London across the water. Dr Johnson stayed and Charles Dickens knew its exterior as a child. On the river in 1989, between Cannon Street and Southwark Bridges, the *Marchioness* pleasure craft sank after hitting the sand dredger *Bowbelle*.

Continue along the waterside to the Financial Times building and go under Southwark Bridge.

Southwark Bridge The 1920s bridge replaces the 1819 toll crossing featured in Charles Dickens' *Little Dorrit*. At the upstream north end is Vintners' Hall, rebuilt in 1992 to a design inspired by St Peter's Rome.

Between Southwark and the Millennium bridges is the riverside associated with the theatre.

Bear Gardens has a ferryman's seat and leads to the site of the Hope Theatre, which staged bear baiting and plays in Elizabeth I's reign. Ben Jonson's *Bartholomew Fair* was premiered in 1614. At the far end is Park Street where the Rose Theatre and the original Globe stood (left).

The Globe is a reconstruction, completed in 1996, of Shakespeare's theatre, which stood nearby (behind the FT) in Park Street from 1599 to 1644. The Bishop of Winchester was willing to let out his parkland for actors, unlike the hostile City of London opposite.

Cardinal Cap Alley is the last of the medieval passages leading from the river. Next door is the Deanery, the Dean of Southwark's residence, and the only deanery to have a view of the wrong cathedral.

Continue under the Millennium Bridge to pass Tate Modern.

Tate Modern, a power station by Giles Gilbert Scott, converted by Swiss architects Herzog and de Meuron, was opened by the Queen in 2000 as the UK's major gallery of modern and contemporary art. The Millennium Bridge outside eventually opened the following year after complaints about its stability.

Follow the promenade towards the Founders Arms and Blackfriars Station at Blackfriars Bridges.

Blackfriars Bridges abut the former Paris Garden mentioned in Shakespeare's play *Henry VIII*. The first road bridge, opened in 1769, was named William Pitt Bridge, but people preferred 'Blackfriars' after the monastery once on the north side. There the River Fleet emerges under the present 1869 bridge, below the spot where Italian banker Robert Calvi was found hanged in 1982. The railway bridge dates from 1884. Between the two are the piers of the first railway bridge, erected in 1862 to carry the main continental

Millennium Bridge

Blackfriars Bridge and the City of London

trains and demolished in 1985. Its fine insignia survives in front of Ludgate House, standing on the site of the burned-out (1803) Albion flour mill, which may have been the inspiration for the 'dark satanic mills' in Blake's hymn *Jerusalem*. Doggett's Coat and Badge, named after the annual rowing race which has passed here since 1715, opened in 1977.

Beyond Doggett's, walk along King's Reach to Oxo Tower Wharf and the gardens.

Follow the Queen's Walk to pass the London Television Centre and the National Theatre.

London Television Centre was home to Carlton, LWT and GMTV. ITV's *This Morning* has a live river backdrop. The *London Today/Tonight* news studio was here until 2004, but ITV continues to have the panoramic backdrop from a live camera feed. The site was a timber yard in the 1840s. Across the water is the Temple with Somerset House to the west. Moored at Temple steps is the 1927 Port of London Authority survey ship *St Katharine*.

Continue to Waterloo Bridge which cuts through the South Bank Centre.

OXO TOWER WHARF

The tower was built in 1930 as London's second highest commercial building, with the OXO windows avoiding planning restrictions on advertising. The main building is older and was once known as River Plate Wharf. The top floor is now a Harvey Nichols restaurant. Members of the public may visit the public viewing section of the roof terrace. Immediately upstream is Old Barge House Stairs, recalling Henry VIII's boatsheds and marking the end of the Paris Garden, whose boundary can be traced along Broadwall inland from the *Hello!* magazine offices. Bernie Spain Gardens, immediately west and replacing Nelson's Wharf and Eldorado's ice-cream factory, is named after local campaigner Bernadette Spain who died in 1984 – the year Coin Street Community Builders was formed to save the OXO Tower and replace 13 acres of derelict land with co-op housing. The riverside walk was opened by the Queen in 1988 when she walked from here to the Royal Festival Hall.

The first **Waterloo Bridge** opened in 1817, having been planned as Strand Bridge before the battle in 1815. The present bridge by Giles Gilbert Scott was built in the late 1930s, complete with explosion chambers in case of invasion.

The South Bank Centre embraces the National Theatre, the National Film Theatre, the Hayward Gallery and the Royal Festival Hall. The latter, built for the 1951 Festival of Britain, is on the site of the Red Lion Brewery, which for a time used river water. Until 1962 a 140ft lead-shot tower, which produced shot for cartridges (1829–1948), stood at the north end of the Festival Hall. The view is of the Savoy.

Go under Hungerford Bridge to pass Jubilee Gardens, the London Eye and County Hall.

Hungerford Bridge was a Brunel suspension bridge, opened in 1845 and sold in 1859 to the London SE Railway, when a foot crossing was included as a planning condition. The railway claimed that few used it in summer due to the river's stench. Brunel's brick piers remain, but the chains were removed to complete his Clifton suspension bridge in Bristol. The present walkways were opened in 2003.

Jubilee Gardens, created in the jubilee year of 1977, was part of the Festival of Britain site. In the 17th century it was a beach reclaimed for willow beds and an asparagus garden.

County Hall, containing flats, two hotels, the London Dungeon and an aquarium, was completed in 1933, after over 20 years' building, to be home of the London County Council (GLC from 1965) until 1985. The site once included Crosse and Blackwell Wharf. The London Eye, the 'Millennium Wheel', was erected in 2000.

Just before the lion, a tunnel takes the path under Westminster Bridge.

Westminster Bridge opened in 1750 despite attempted sabotage by ferrymen. The present bridge, complementing the Victorian Gothic Houses of Parliament, opened in 1861. The lion comes from the top of the Lion Brewery on the Festival Hall site.

Follow the Albert Embankment in front of the hospital with a fine view of the Houses of Parliament.

St Thomas' Hospital, founded in Southwark by the monks of Southwark Priory, is dedicated to both St Thomas Becket and St Thomas the Apostle – so 'Thomas" is pronounced 'Thomases'. The hospital moved here to reclaimed land in 1871, with the original buildings being based on a French hospital visited by Florence Nightingale. A museum named after her is in the new building.

Just before Lambeth Bridge there is Lambeth Palace.

Lambeth Palace has been the Archbishop of Canterbury's official residence since 1197. The gatehouse was built in 1495. The adjoining St Mary-at-Lambeth Church is now the Garden Museum. Charles I's gardener John Tradescant and his son, who brought many now popular plants to England, are buried in the churchyard along with Captain Bligh of mutiny on the *Bounty* fame.

    Lambeth Bridge succeeded the archbishop's horseferry (hence Horseferry Road opposite), used by Queen Mary and her baby (the Old Pretender) when fleeing abroad in 1688. The ferry ceased when Westminster Bridge opened and a bridge here (foot toll ½d) was not built until 1861. The present crossing, completed in 1932, is decorated with the pineapples introduced to England by John Tradescant the Younger. On the upstream north end is MI5's HQ, identified by radio masts.

The path runs under the bridge to join the road in front of the International Maritime Organisation and fire station which has a pier for fireboats. Opposite is the Tate Pier and Tate Britain.

Tate Britain, the original Tate Gallery and now the national gallery of British art from 1500, opened in 1897 with 67 paintings. It was the gift of sugar magnate Henry Tate and stands on the site of the Millbank Penitentiary, which had been erected on the marshy land in 1821. The pier, designed by London Eye inventors David Marks and Julia Barfield, opened in 2003.

Stay by the river as the road veers away at Peninsula Heights. Beyond Lack's Drawdock the path is in front of MI6's Vauxhall Cross building. Go under Vauxhall Bridge and up the slope to St George Wharf.

Walk along St George Wharf. Soon the path is parallel to Nine Elms Lane. Between two blocks of flats, where the path is known as William Henry Way, is Elm Quay.

VAUXHALL BRIDGE

Vauxhall Bridge was opened in 1816 as Regent's Bridge, but at the turn of the century was replaced by the present structure decorated with bronze figures. The River Effra, which rises in Norwood and gives its name to Brixton's Effra Road, flows unseen under the path between the bridge and the huge M16 building by Terry Farrell, called Vauxhall Cross (but also known as 'Spooksville') and completed in 1993. 'Vauxhall' is derived from 'Faulkes Hall', built in about 1200 for Faulkes de Breaute. Between 1660 and 1859 Vauxhall was well known for the pleasure garden lying between Golding Street, Laud Street, Kennington Lane and St Oswald Place. In 1864 the Pearson-designed St Peter's Church was built next to the manager's house, which became the vicarage. The altar marks the site of Neptune's Fountain. A rural air is now maintained by the city farm within the garden boundary. Doulton Pottery was founded in Vauxhall Walk in 1815 and remained until 1956. Brunswick House, near the river, was built in 1758 by the Dawson family who ran a timber wharf behind.

Elm Quay has a representation of Old Father Thames by Stephen Duncan, completed in 1988. Behind can be seen the new USA Embassy. William Henry Walk is named after Wandsworth's Borough Engineer who died in 1988. A river footbridge is planned at this point which would lead to Pimlico Gardens. Nearby is Dolphin Square, Europe's biggest block of flats, completed in 1937.

Continue by the river until the path turns inland to the road. Go right to a row of tall buildings. Walk between the first two to reach Tideway Walk.

The Battersea barge **Maria**, built in Holland in 1931, carried grain on the Seine until she was seized by the Nazis. In 1979 she crossed the Channel to first become a floating restaurant at Lymington in Hampshire before coming up the Thames in 1987. Coal barges used to unload here at Nine Elms Pier for Vauxhall Gasworks until 1971. A regular visitor was the sand dredger *Bowbelle*.

Beyond the pier, the path comes up against an aggregates wharf and Battersea Power Station, forcing an inland diversion. Go down Kirtling Street and left to the main road. Turn right to keep on the main Battersea Park Road over the railway and past Battersea Dogs' Home to bear right along Prince of Wales Drive. At the roundabout cross the end of Queenstown Road (leading to Chelsea Bridge) to enter Battersea Park. Bear right to find the undergrowth of the Wilderness blocking out sight and sound of the traffic. On reaching the river bear left to join the path leading to Albert Bridge at the far end.

Battersea Park opened in 1853 after the marshland had been raised with soil from the new Royal Victoria Dock downstream. The Buddhist peace pagoda was erected in 1985. The riverside path has a view of Chelsea and its Royal Hospital – the gap in the houses is the once-waterside Chelsea Physic Garden.

Albert Bridge had its strength questioned just 11 years after its 1873 opening, but it has survived, with its central prop eventually added in 1973. The only other example of this rigid chain design is in Prague. The toll booths, closed since 1879, and the 3000 bulbs which illuminate the bridge at night, give a seaside pier appearance.

Cross the road to find the path continuing by the toll booth. Chelsea Old Church is across the water. Beyond Ransom Dock Entrance pass architect Norman Foster's in-house-designed glass office, opened in 1990, and his Albion Riverside flats, completed in 2004, alongside Battersea Bridge.

The first **bridge** at Battersea was a 1771 wooden structure called 'Chelsea Bridge' and then 'Old Chain Bridge' which replaced a 200-year-old ferry. Painters Turner and Whistler both depict the bridge, which was succeeded by the present one in 1890.

Cross the road to follow Morgan's Walk to the Montevetro Building.

Morgan's Walk is alongside the former Morgan Crucible works which had a clocktower featured in Whistler's 'Nocturne' series. Opposite are Chelsea's famous houseboats (rising twice a day with the tide) and London Transport's Lots Road Power Station, built in 1905 to supply the District Line.

The **Montevetro Building**, designed by Richard Rogers and containing a 100 apartments, was completed in 1999. The name is Italian for 'glass mountain'. The site was occupied by the Hovis Flour Mill, built in 1887, and grain arrived by barge for the next century. The mill was sold in 1994 and demolition followed in 1997. The first mill was built in 1794.

Continue into the riverside churchyard of Battersea Old Church.

The window commemorating William Blake's wedding at **Battersea Old Church** (six years after the church was rebuilt in 1776) was dedicated in the presence of former prime minister Harold Wilson in 1979. The Curtis window includes a map showing lost riverside gardens. Turner often painted sunsets from the west room where the view is now of Chelsea Harbour, begun in 1986 on the site of a railway goods yard. Cargo was unloaded in Chelsea Creek, which is the borough boundary, so the development (where Michael Caine, Tom Stoppard and Elton John were early residents) is in Fulham and not Chelsea.

Pass the drawdock and at once turn right to rejoin the river. When the flats end there is a view of Old Battersea House.

Old Battersea House, built in 1899, was recently the home of American publisher Malcolm Forbes who lent it to ex-President Ronald Reagan. Forbes' son inherited the house, which contained a fine art collection and, Forbes believed, the ghost of an old lady.

The path passes along Albion Quay before joining a road and running under a railway bridge.

Battersea Railway Bridge opened in 1863 to carry both standard and GWR broad-gauge trains between Clapham and Willesden junctions.

After passing Lombard Wharf go right to reach the river at Regent Wharf. Cross a drawbridge to Falcon Wharf and follow the path inland down the side of Battersea Heliport. At a road go right and just past the Crown Plaza turn back to the river. Continue upstream to pass Price's Court which is built on a candle factory

Price's Candles began here in 1830 by making cheap candles using coconuts which arrived by barge. In 1840 many houses lit a Price's candle in the window to celebrate Queen Victoria's wedding. Today there is a candle shop, but the factory is now housing. York Place is a reminder that in Tudor times the site was the Archbishop of York's London residence, with water on two sides – the Falcon Brook flowed into the now disappeared Battersea Creek on the downstream side.

Pass the end of Cotton Row to reach Plantation Wharf.

Plantation Wharf was built as an office development but went into receivership before being turned into flats in 1993. Once, sugar cane was landed here from barges sent up from the docks – hence Molasses House. Adjoining were Mendip and Sherwood timber wharves. Immediately downstream is Gargoyle Wharf, home until 1989 of Wandsworth Distillery, which has been redeveloped as residential Battersea Reach.

Continue over former timber wharves to go on to Battersea Reach where the new path is set back to allow for tidal planting. Pass the Waterfront pub and at the far end bear left to find a tunnel under Wandsworth Bridge.

Continue ahead along the cobbled Pier Terrace to the junction with Jews Row. The sign of the 24-hour McDonald's can be seen to the left. Opposite is the Ship Inn.

The Ship Inn, opened about 1786, nearly closed in 1981, but 10 years later it was Pub of the Year. The sign shows the ship on which Sir Allen Young (of Young's Brewery fame) explored the North-West Passage in the 1870s. The land immediately upstream was a gasworks, and Nichols Walk promenade is on the line of a travelling crane which ran between the river and a large coal bunker belonging to the gasworks. Downstream Pier Wharf alongside the pub remains a working wharf for unloading gravel.

Go ahead down the side of the pub to reach Nichols Walk. At the far end the path runs above the Refuse Transfer Station to the River Wandle.

The **refuse transfer station** opened in 1984, the most advanced in Europe. 4000 tons of refuse are taken downstream by water to Belvedere each week. A century ago this site was Feathers Wharf with an inn and tea garden.

Until the high path running above the refuse station is opened, walkers must go left down Waterside Path – the pepperpot tower of St Anne's Wandsworth can be seen ahead. Go right along Smugglers Way at the back of the refuse station on a road which becomes the Causeway and crosses the River Wandle.

The **River Wandle**, which rises in Croydon and features in Izaak Walton's *The Compleat Angler*, gives its name to Wandsworth. There was a corn tidemill here at the Wandle's mouth in the mid 1760s. Above the first road bridge the riverbank was the oldest brewing site in Britain until Young's closed in 2006. Brewing began in 1581 with coal and malt arriving by barge. Dray horses were stabled here until very recently.

Keep forward over Causeway Island and Bell Lane Creek to turn right. (If the path in front of Riverside Quarter is closed keep ahead to Sainsbury's and turn right to pass between buildings to river.) Pass Point Pleasant where the Cat's Back pub and Prospect House can be seen.

Prospect House was built about 1805 for Joseph Gattey, owner of a nearby vinegar works. The road known as Point Pleasant existed in the 1730s. Prospect Quay, formerly a Calor Gas depot with a jetty, was developed in 1996 as flats with an extended pier for houseboats. Immediately downstream is Riverside Quarter, on the site of the former Shell Oil Terminal.

Go ahead past Venetian-style moorings at Prospect Quay to enter Wandsworth Park.

Wandsworth Park opened in 1903 on the remains of North Field, which had an old riverside path. Across the river is Hurlingham House, built in 1760 and now occupied by the Hurlingham Club. In 1875 the first polo match was played on the lawn.

At the far end of the park leave the river to go through a gated archway behind the houses and pass through Blade Mews into Deodar Road.

Prospect Quay at Wandsworth

Deodar Road has Putney's only riverside houses. Writer Edna O'Brien lived at number 87 and *Desert Island Discs* creator Roy Plomley at 91. The road is crossed by the District Line bridge, opened in 1889, which has a pedestrian link to Putney Bridge Underground Station on the far bank.

At the T-junction at the far end go right and walk down the side of a house to reach the river. Pass the Boathouse pub, a former vinegar brewery, and Brewhouse Street drawdock to reach Putney Wharf. Turn into Church Square to pass behind the church and reach Putney High Street and Putney Bridge.

FACILITIES INFORMATION – TOWER BRIDGE TO PUTNEY

Refreshments
Southwark Cathedral: Refectory. 9am–6pm (weekends 10am–6pm).
Lambeth Bridge: Lambeth Pier café. 8am–5pm.
Wandsworth Bridge: McDonald's. Open 24 hours.
Wandsworth Bridge: The Ship. 11am–11pm. Food all day.

Accommodation
Blackfriars Bridge: City YHA, Carter Lane (near St Paul's Cathedral),
    EC4 5AB (0845 371 9012, www.yha.org.uk).
Bankside: The Anchor (Premier Inn), SE1 9EF (0870 9906402,
    www.premierinn.com).
Wandsworth: Holiday Inn Express, Smugglers Way, SW18 1EG
    (0871 423 4876, www.hiexpress.com).

Transport
Tower Bridge: Underground to Tower Hill.
Vauxhall: Underground and National Rail.
Putney: National Rail or Underground from Putney Bridge (on left bank).

Map
OS Explorer 161 (London South) and 173 (London North).

STAGE 3
Putney to Kingston

Start	Putney Bridge
Finish	Kingston Bridge
Distance	13 miles (20.9km)

This section takes the path out of urban London and past several fine riverside mansions and gardens, including Kew Gardens. Putney is the start of the towpath which runs as far as Inglesham in Wiltshire and is also the Thames Path for most of the way. Beyond Putney's boundary, marked by Beverley Brook, the environment is rural. Birds seen here include grey herons, coots and plenty of Canada geese. Cormorants are common around Chiswick. At Teddington the river ceases to be tidal.

PUTNEY

The landmark church tower is 15th century. The church's Bishop West Chapel recalls the local baker's son who became Bishop of Ely and Catherine of Aragon's chaplain. Thomas Cromwell, who took Henry VIII's side and implemented the Reformation, was also born here. Later, Thomas's relative Oliver Cromwell chaired the Putney Debates in the church – a plaque (south side) records this first public discussion of democratic principles which influenced the drafting of the US constitution. At this time the Roundheads threw a pontoon bridge across to Fulham. When the first permanent bridge was erected in 1729, running from behind the church, it was the only road crossing between Kingston and London Bridge. The present bridge dates from 1886. Historian Edward Gibbon was baptised in the church in 1737, and a century later Charles Dickens is thought to have had this building in mind when he described David Copperfield's wedding. Lewis Carroll often stayed with his uncle at Park Lodge next to the almshouses in Putney Bridge Road.

For 1:25K route map see booklet pages 72–78.

From the south end of Putney Bridge walk upstream along Lower Richmond Road and turn on to the Embankment. Just before the pier there is a bollard marked UBR indicating the University Boat Race start. Continue past the

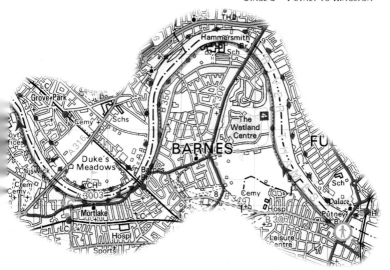

Duke's Head to reach the rowing clubs and boathouses. (Behind trees opposite is Fulham Palace, the Bishop of London's residence from 1141 to 1973, where England's longest moat was fed by the river.) The road ends at Leaders Gardens just before Beverley Brook.

Map continues on page 52

Beverley Brook flows down from Richmond Park to serve here as the Wandsworth–Richmond borough boundary – once the London–Surrey border. Here, in the creek mouth, Putney's rubbish was tipped into barges to go down the Thames. Almost opposite is Fulham football ground, known as 'Craven Cottage' after a picturesque riverside villa which stood on the site from 1780 until it was burnt down in 1888.

At once the towpath has a rural feel as it passes bushes and old ash trees alongside Barn Elms playing fields. Beyond the Queen Elizabeth Walk turning, the towpath runs below Barn Elms Wetlands where there is the Boat Race mile post.

51

Map continues
on page 54

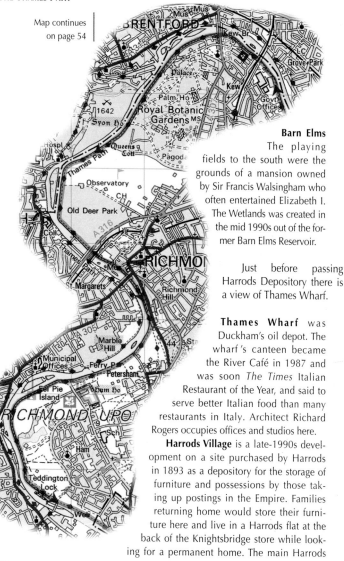

Barn Elms
The playing fields to the south were the grounds of a mansion owned by Sir Francis Walsingham who often entertained Elizabeth I. The Wetlands was created in the mid 1990s out of the former Barn Elms Reservoir.

Just before passing Harrods Depository there is a view of Thames Wharf.

Thames Wharf was Duckham's oil depot. The wharf's canteen became the River Café in 1987 and was soon *The Times* Italian Restaurant of the Year, and said to serve better Italian food than many restaurants in Italy. Architect Richard Rogers occupies offices and studios here.

Harrods Village is a late-1990s development on a site purchased by Harrods in 1893 as a depository for the storage of furniture and possessions by those taking up postings in the Empire. Families returning home would store their furniture here and live in a Harrods flat at the back of the Knightsbridge store while looking for a permanent home. The main Harrods

Depository building on the riverside, completed in 1914, is a familiar landmark on the Boat Race course, but its similar silhouette to the Brompton Road store causes confusion in the minds of some television viewers when the commentator speaks of crews 'passing Harrods'. Immediately behind is the Charles Harrod Building, a former soap factory and the original depository. The Richard Burbidge Building was a candle factory.

Beyond here there is a view of the new Fulham Reach tall flats downstream of the Riverside Studios.

Fulham Reach is on the site of Brandenburgh House where Queen Caroline lived during George IV's attempts to divorce her. Watermen took the Queen's side and held a massive demonstration of support here on the water. The Queen died at the house in 1821 just a year after being refused entry to her husband's coronation. The following year the mansion was demolished.

Pass under Hammersmith Bridge.

The first **suspension bridge** was built at Hammersmith in the 1820s by William Tierney Clark, who went on to build Marlow Bridge and is buried in St Paul's Hammersmith where the memorial stone bears the outline of a bridge. The first bridge is seen in Walter Greaves' painting *Hammersmith Bridge on Boat Race Day*. The present bridge was erected in 1883–7 using the original piers and abutments.

Soon there is a view across to Hammersmith Pier.

Hammersmith Pier marks a filled-in creek. Alongside is the Dove a 17th-century coffee house turned pub featured in AP Herbert's novel *The Water Gipsies*. Just upstream is four-storey

Kelmscott House, home of William Morris, whose country house was riverside Kelmscott Manor in Oxfordshire. In August 1880 he took a week sailing upstream to his second home.

The towpath bends south past St Paul's School grounds to draw level with Chiswick across the water.

Chiswick is partly hidden by Chiswick Eyot, planted with willows once cut to make fish baskets. ('Eyot' or 'ait' means 'small river island'.) Just visible behind the upstream end is Fuller's Brewery, which used to land hops and malt by barge. Fishermen lived in cottages near the Church Drawdock, which had a ferry until 1934. Artist William Hogarth is buried in front of the church and James Whistler is in the cemetery. Upstream is residential Church Wharf, once occupied by Thornycroft shipbuilding, which moved to Southampton in 1904 when destroyers became too large to pass under bridges, and Corney Reach (with pier) on the site of Corney House visited by Elizabeth I in 1602.

The towpath is alongside the Leg O'Mutton nature reserve before merging with the road at Barnes.

Barnes Church, largely rebuilt after the 1978 fire in which the 16th-century tower survived with the clock in working order, was consecrated in 1215 by Archbishop Langton on his way back from securing King John's assent to Magna Carta at upstream Runnymede. Opposite the pond is Milbourne House where novelist Henry Fielding lived – the Georgian façade hides an Elizabethan building.

Chiswick church

Composer Gustav Holst lived at 10 The Terrace (by the river) where he wrote *The Planets* suite in the main bedroom. The railway bridge dates from 1846, with the footbridge attached in 1895 strong enough to hold a Boat Race crowd.

Where the road leaves the river continue on the towpath behind Ye White Hart and along the Mortlake waterfront, passing the brewery by the drawdock, to the Ship at Thames Bank.

Mortlake is famous for its tapestries, including those now at Hampton Court, made here from 1619 to 1703 by Flemish weavers. Budweiser is now produced on the site, continuing the brewery association begun in the 19th century when hops and coal arrived by barge. The much-restored church retains its Tudor tower – the bells were rung whenever Elizabeth I passed on the river between London and Richmond. The Ship was once the Boat Race finishing point. Nearby Chiswick Bridge was built in 1933.

Pass the Boat Race finishing post to go under the bridge. For the next mile the path is alongside confusingly named Kew Riverside housing development. Across the water are Grove Park backgardens. After passing under Kew Railway Bridge there is a view of Oliver's Ait and Strand-on-the-Green.

Strand-on-the-Green was a cluster of fishermen's cottages until the 1770s. Painter John Zoffany lived at Zoffany House (the blue plaque can just be seen) from 1780 to 1810, and in his *Last Supper* he modelled the apostles on local fishermen and Judas on a churchwarden at Kew – so the painting has ended up in St Paul's Brentford rather than Kew church. The house was once the home of television writer Carla Lane. The bridge carrying the District Line opened in 1869.

Pass under Kew Bridge to reach Kew.

Kew Bridge was renamed Edward VII Bridge when the present structure was opened by the King in 1903, but the original name first used in 1759 has stuck. The main road runs across the green, with the church where the late Queen Mary's parents married after her father proposed in the gardens. The mausoleum at the east end held the remains (now at Windsor) of her grandparents, the Duke and Duchess of Cambridge, who lived at Cambridge Cottage. Painter Thomas Gainsborough is buried outside the church's south wall, while Zoffany is on the east side. In Kew Road the Maids of Honour teashop bakes cakes to a secret recipe used for Henry VIII. On the far bank is the 1867 tower of a pumping station (now Kew Bridge Steam Museum) which had river water pumped up it to run down into the mains.

The river is divided by islands.

Brentford Ait was planted with trees in the 1920s to screen Brentford's gasworks. In the gap (known as Hog Hole) between the two islands can be seen St George's Brentford (now the Musical Museum). The third island is a former osier ground where barges were repaired until 1980.

After a short distance the path is in front of Kew Palace and Kew Gardens.

Kew Palace, built in Dutch style in 1631, is the smallest royal palace. George III spent his last years here when the garden was subject to flooding. His wife Queen Charlotte died here in 1818 and in the same year Queen Victoria's parents were married in the drawing room which has several Zoffany portraits. (Admission via Kew Gardens and additional ticket needed.)

Kew Gardens, the Royal Botanic Gardens, was founded in 1759 by Princess Augusta whose greenhouse is now the Orangery. Her landmark pagoda was decorated with dragons until the Prince Regent pawned them to pay debts. Entry via Brentford Ferry Gate – the ferry ceased operation in 1939. Open 9.30am–6.30pm (dusk in winter); admission charge.

There is a view over the river to Brentford before Syon House comes into view across the north bank meadows.

The riverside Pavilion at Isleworth

In **Brentford**, during the 17th century bricks, fruit and fish went to London by barges which returned with horse-dung ballast used as fertiliser – there was a Dung Wharf. The River Brent (Grand Union Canal) joins here. Just upstream is Brentford Dock, which was completed in 1859 and closed in 1964.

Syon House, home of the Duke of Northumberland, whose lion crest can be seen on the roof, is on the site of a convent founded in 1431. The huge abbey church was destroyed during the Reformation upheaval. The community moved abroad and was later in Devon until closure in 2011. Lady Jane Grey made her bid to oust Mary I from here, and Charles I, while a prisoner at Hampton Court, came by water to see his children. In 1616 Pocahontas, who found London rather dirty, was loaned the country house. The tide meadow and its natural creeks are washed twice daily by freshwater pushed back by the tide. In 1642 the Battle of Brentford was fought to the north when Royalists took the town, slashing fishing nets and driving defenders into the Thames. The Civil War might have ended by agreement the next day at Turnham Green, but for the sound of an ammunition barge being blown up here by Royalists, which was mistaken for gunfire.

The towpath soon runs alongside Old Deer Park and across the old meridian marked on the ground.

Old Deer Park is the former Richmond Palace (see below) parkland where George III built an observatory for Sir William Chambers. The obelisks are on an old meridian used to determine time prior to Greenwich Mean Time.

Soon the river bends at the ferry for Isleworth village on the far bank.

The church at **Isleworth** is modern but retains its 15th-century tower. Bodies of Great Plague victims were brought here by barge and buried behind the church. The 500-year-old London Apprentice pub recalls the apprentices who rowed up from the City on their annual day off. In the late 20th century many Westminster politicians came to the Ferry House,

The old meridian at Richmond

where Turner lived, for Lord Gilmour's annual garden party, described as 'the Goodwood of the
political season' and once causing a government's
Commons majority to fall to four. The downstream
pink residence is a Tudor boathouse converted during the Georgian period into a teahouse. The ferry,
restored in 1995 after a 32-year gap which had seen
an attempted revival in 1983 fail, operates occasionally at weekends; small charge.

Stay on the towpath still alongside the tree-lined Old
Deer Park with modern Isleworth hidden by Isleworth
Ait. On turning southeast there is Richmond Half-Tide
Weir and the first lock (which saves Richmond from a
dramatic drop in water level at low tide). Cross the old
meridian again and beyond two bridges is Richmond's
first house.

RICHMOND-UPON-THAMES

Richmond-upon-Thames was West Sheen until Henry VII named his
palace here after his earldom derived from Yorkshire's Richmond.
Mary I and Philip of Spain honeymooned here and Elizabeth I died
here. The gatehouse and courtyard can be found off Water Lane.
Maids of Honour Row was built in 1724 for the Princess of Wales'
ladies-in-waiting, but the last monarch to live here was Charles I,
whose chaplain founded the almshouses in the Vineyard. Actor
Edmund Kean is buried in the church, having had his body refused by
Westminster Abbey due to a drunken reputation. A plaque in Paradise
Street marks the house where Leonard and Virginia Woolf started the
Hogarth Press on the kitchen table. Richmond Bridge was built in
1777 when it cost ½d to cross and 1d if pushing a wheelbarrow. The
neo-classical development next to the bridge is by Quinlan Terry.

Go under the bridge to pass Richmond Landing
Stage. The towpath briefly swings away from the water-
side before returning at Chitty Hole to run alongside
Petersham Meadows below Richmond Hill. Pass Glover's
Island and the end of Petersham's River Lane.

The church across the meadows at **Petersham** is partly Norman and has box pews. Weddings here have included Prince Rupert in 1664 and the Queen Mother's parents in 1881. George Vancouver, who discovered Vancouver Island and lived at River Lane's Navigator's Cottage, is buried by the churchyard's south wall. Cows grazing on the meadows are the nearest to central London.

After 400 yards Marble Hill House can be seen on the far bank.

Marble Hill House was completed in 1729 for George II's mistress Lady Suffolk, and in 1795 Mrs Fitzherbert, the Prince Regent's first wife, lived there. Hammerton's Ferry, which can be hailed from the steps, was started in 1909 by Walter Hammerton. Fourth owner Francis Spencer operates an electric Peace of Mind ferry (built in 1997 at Teddington) at weekends 10am–6.30pm (or dusk if earlier) and daily Feb-Oct 10am–6pm; small charge.

Soon Ham House is seen in a gap in the trees to the left.

Ham House, built in 1610, is little changed since the Earl of Lauderdale (the L in Charles II's 'cabal cabinet') and his wife made it their home after marrying at Petersham church. Soon after, John Evelyn wrote that Ham 'is indeed inferior to few of the best villas in Italy itself; the House furnished like a great Prince's; the Park with Flower Gardens, Orangeries, Groves, Avenues, Courts, Statues, Perspectives, Fountains, Aviaries and all this on the banks of the sweetest river in the World ...'. The garden is a rare survival of the formal 17th-century style. Ham House is in the care of the National Trust, which encourages visitors to arrive either on foot or by boat as in the 17th century. Ham House is open Apr-Oct Sat-Wed 1–5pm and the garden Sat–Wed 11am–6pm (or dusk); admission charges.

Just before passing a car park there is a glimpse across the water of 18th-century Orleans House' octagon garden room. Ahead is Eel Pie Island, blocking the view of Twickenham.

TWICKENHAM

Eel Pie Island, once Twickenham Ayt, is named after a dish served on the island from the 16th century, sampled by Henry VIII and later served at the now demolished Eel Pie Island Hotel, which opened in 1830. The two-acre island was a well-known picnic spot, featured by Charles Dickens in *Nicholas Nickleby*, where he writes of 'a cold collation, bottled beer, shrub, and shrimp and to dance in the open air to the music of a locomotive band'. In the sixties the hotel was popular for its pop concerts featuring the Rolling Stones. Today's 300 residents include a community of artists and Trevor Bayliss, who lives in the self-built house where he invented the clockwork radio. Before the move to plastic, the University Boat Race boats were made in the boatyard on the north side. The island was served by ferry until 1956, when the toll bridge (2d until decimalization) linked to the Twickenham bank was built.

Alexander Pope, who lived in a riverside house (demolished), is buried in the church in Twickenham which has a 14th-century tower. The vicarage was once home of tea merchant Thomas Twining. In 1958 the CND symbol was designed by local resident Gerald Holtom for the Aldermaston March. Upstream of the island, as the river begins to bend, there is a view of St James School which includes Pope's Grotto, where the poet entertained satirist Jonathan Swift.

The river turns south and between a dock entrance and Teddington there is the Boundary Stone.

The **Boundary Stone** erected in 1909 marks the division between the downstream Port of London Authority and the Environment Agency (formerly Thames Conservancy), which is the controlling authority for upstream navigation.

The tidal Thames ends at the lock which takes its name from the village of **Teddington** on the far bank reached by a long footbridge. The parish church dates from the 16th century, but the landmark is St Alban's, known as 'the Thames Valley cathedral', and based on Clermont-Ferrard Cathedral after the vicar visiting with a church-warden exclaimed: 'If only we could have a church like that!' Built in 1887–9 it had Fr Alfred Hope Patten, who restored the Shrine of Our Lady at Walsingham, as curate, and playwright Noel Coward, born at 131 Waldegrave Road, in the choir. The huge church was declared redundant in 1977. RD Blackmore wrote *Lorna Doone* in the 1860s while living on the site of Doone Close. By the river was the Warner Brothers film studios, which is now a housing development. Teddington is also the end of the dual Thames Path route which begins at the Greenwich foot tunnel.

Soon there is a view on the Teddington bank down Broom Water.

Broom Water was a natural creek extended three times its length in 1863 as a waterside housing development.

At Half Mile Tree the towpath is on a riverside road before running under a long line of trees on the edge of Canbury Gardens.

Canbury Gardens was marshland known as the Eyots until the dumping of building waste led to draining for a park in 1889. However, the prom-enade became known as 'perfume parade' due to smells from a fertiliser factory. Immediately to the south, between 1947 and 1994 the riverside land-mark was Kingston Power Station.

Go under a railway bridge, past Turk's Pier, on to a promenade and under Kingston Bridge. At once go left up a slope to reach the town and cross the bridge.

FACILITIES INFORMATION – PUTNEY TO KINGSTON

Refreshments
Putney Bridge: St Mary's Church café. 8am–5pm; Sun 11am–6pm.
Putney towpath: Looloo's, Leaders Gardens. 11am–5.30pm.
Kew: Maids of Honour teashop, Kew Road. 8.30am–6pm.
Kew: St Anne's Church, Kew Green. Teas on summer Sun afternoons.
Canbury Gardens, Kingston: Boaters Inn on the riverside. 11am–11pm.

Accommodation
Kew: Maids of Honour teashop, Kew Road TW9 3DU (020 8940 2752,
www.theoriginalmaidsofhonour.co.uk)

Transport
Putney: Underground to Putney Bridge (on left bank) or National Rail to Putney.
Kew Bridge: Underground and National Rail from Kew Gardens or National
Rail from Kew Bridge (left bank).
Richmond: Underground and National Rail.
Kingston: National Rail.

Map
OS Explorer 161 (London South).

STAGE 4
Kingston to Chertsey

Start	Kingston Bridge
Finish	Chertsey Bridge
Distance	11 miles (17.7km)

At Kingston the towpath crosses to the left bank for the first time. Beyond Hampton Court, on the edge of the county of London, the towpath switches back to the right bank as far as Shepperton. Walkers should note that the last ferry at Shepperton is at 6pm in summer and earlier in winter (see below). An alternative waymarked route, handy for those wishing to use Shepperton Station, can be followed across Walton Bridge.

For 1:25K route map see booklet pages 66–72.

Map continues on page 68

Cross Kingston Bridge and turn left down Barge Walk to reach the riverbank. Opposite can be seen the Hogsmill River, which rises near

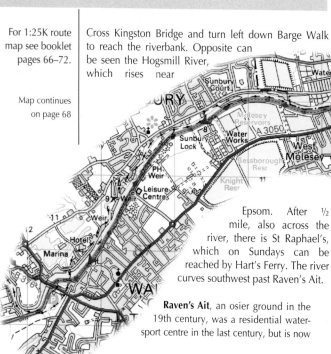

Epsom. After ½ mile, also across the river, there is St Raphael's, which on Sundays can be reached by Hart's Ferry. The river curves southwest past Raven's Ait.

Raven's Ait, an osier ground in the 19th century, was a residential watersport centre in the last century, but is now a venue for conferences, receptions and weddings. The name derivation is uncertain, but Seething Wells on the far bank recalls therapeutic springs there.

The path continues alongside Hampton Court Park with views of residential Seething Wells and Thames Ditton on the far bank.

Thames Ditton Island is now covered by 48 timber houses and bungalows. The village on the right bank behind has a 13th-century church and a riverside inn, the Olde Swan.

Here by the towpath is the Pavilion.

The **Pavilion**, designed by Wren and built in 1700 for William III's entertaining, has been the home

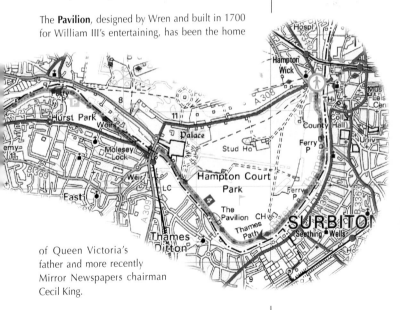

of Queen Victoria's father and more recently Mirror Newspapers chairman Cecil King.

As the path comes level with Hampton Court Palace's Privy Garden there is a view across to the River Mole, which rises near Gatwick Airport.

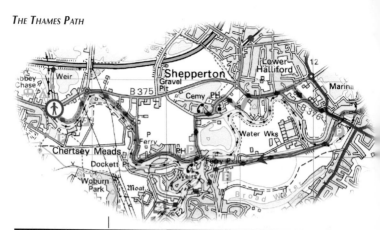

KINGSTON-UPON-THAMES

Alfred chose to be crowned here in an attempt to unite Mercia (left bank) with the Saxons against the Danes who later came up river. Six Saxon kings, including Ethelred the Unready, were crowned on the Coronation Stone outside the Guildhall. The Roman ford was replaced with a bridge by the 12th century. The church has a 14th-century pillar painting of St Blaise (patron of local drapers) and Holy Trinity Chapel, built by the Shipmen's Guild (forerunner of Trinity House). The church was the setting for John Millais' 1863 painting *My First Sermon* and its sequel showing a little girl asleep. Turk's Pier is run by Queen's Waterman Michael Turk, whose ancestor kept a salmon weir near here for Henry VIII. The market operates under a Charles I charter which allows no other within a seven-mile radius. The riverside Bishop out of Residence pub is on the site of a house used in the 14th century by Bishop of Winchester William of Wykeham when travelling between Winchester and Southwark. Borders bookshop has the 'magnificent carved oak staircase' featured in JK Jerome's *Three men in a Boat*. Lloyd's Bank has a plaque to HMV dog Nipper who is buried on the site. The Rose at Kingston theatre was built in 2004 and is based on the Rose at Southwark (see Stage 2).

Hampton Court Palace was a Knights Hospitaller house rebuilt by Cardinal Wolsey to such a size that he needed almost 500 servants. He gave his residence to Henry VIII who brought five of his six wives here – he is said to have been in the tennis court when he heard confirmation of Anne Boleyn's execution downstream at the Tower of London. To the Tudors and Stuarts the river was the main highway, and Charles II was given two gondolas with four gondoliers from Venice for use here. The Vine, the world's oldest and largest, with roots watered by the Thames, was planted in 1765 for George III who never lived here. His son William IV started guided tours and Queen Victoria opened the main rooms for free public viewing. Today the palace is open daily; admission charge.

Walk over Hampton Court Bridge to reach East Molesey.

The first **bridge** at Hampton Court, built in 1753, was Chinese in appearance, having been inspired by the new bridge at Walton (see below). The toll for walkers (½d on weekdays and 1d on Sundays) continued in force for two more structures until 1876. The tollhouse can be seen as part of the Mitre Hotel which, along with the 1865 cast-iron bridge, features in several Alfred Sisley paintings. The castellated abutments of this crossing remain just upstream of its successor, designed by Edwin Lutyens and opened in 1933.

Bridge Street, in **East Molesey**, indicates the line of the old main road before the bridge was realigned. When St Mary's Church was rebuilt in the 1860s, old toll bridge posts were placed at the churchyard entrance to deter body-snatchers who came by river hoping to sell to London medical schools. The Bell, near the church, has 'circa 1450' above the door. The railway station is now called Hampton Court.

Continue upstream along River Bank to a bus stop where a slope leads down to the river. Beyond Molesey Lock and Weir there are Ash and Tagg's islands, with a Swiss cottage seen between the two.

Tagg's Island, once Walnut Tree Island, is named after Royal Waterman Tom Tagg who ran a boatyard and hotel here in the 19th century. Later Fred Karno covered the island with his leisure complex. The Swiss cottage on the Hampton bank was brought from Switzerland in 1899.

Just before the cricket ground there is the Eights Tree memorial to playwright and rower RC Sherriff. Later the towpath is alongside the former Hurst Park Racecourse with a view of Garrick's Temple and Hampton church.

The riverside church at **Hampton**, rebuilt in 1831 with all materials delivered by barge, contains work by *Radio Times* illustrator Eric Fraser, who lived next to the churchyard in the house of Edward VI's childhood nurse. Garrick's Temple, dedicated to Shakespeare, was built in 1755 for actor Richard Garrick who lived in the house behind. Zoffany (see Stage 3) painted Garrick and his wife at the Temple. The ferry has been operating since at least 1519. Hurst Park Racecourse, on the towpath side, closed in 1960.

The long Platt's Eyot (where torpedo boats were built) screens a waterworks. Beyond the island the rising towpath passes riverside homes. At a bend the way is below a long wall hiding reservoirs. On coming level with Grand Junction Island the path passes between wartime defences. After a mile the wall gives way to railings, and across the water Sunbury Court is seen behind Sunbury Court Island. When almost level with the end of the island there is a City of London coal tax post on the West Molesey–Walton parish boundary. Soon Sunbury on the far bank comes into view.

Most of the **Sunbury-on-Thames** is unseen apart from a pub and former boat builders. Sunbury Court, now the Salvation Army Conference Centre, was built in about 1770 as a riverside mansion. Just below Sunbury Lock in the late 18th century was one of several paygates for the towing horses – 3d here but only 2d at Laleham.

After the Weir pub, the towpath is along the almost straight Walton Mile once used for regattas. Soon visible on the far side is a line of chalets on Wheatley's Ait.

Wheatley's Ait was an osier ground until the 1880s. The first residents were a group of bachelors who came at weekends and holidays. Later they allowed women to join them so long as they left by midnight. Now it is a second home to 16 families.

At the far end of the Walton Mile is River House with its public garden, and Walton Wharf at Walton-on-Thames.

Walton Wharf is a former ferry point with the grass approach seen opposite. As early as Tudor times timber was sent to London from here. In the

Riverside homes near Sunbury

19th century coal was unloaded for the gas company, and livestock watered here included the occasional circus elephant. The Anglers was built in 1870. Behind are the Swan, where in 1910 songwriter Jerome Kern first met his wife Eva, the landlord's daughter, and River House, where composer Sir Arthur Sullivan lived between 1894 and 1898.

After a short distance a bridge takes the towpath over a marina entrance. Continue round the double bend to Walton Bridge, where there are occasional diversions.

Walton Bridge was the least attractive on the river, being the second temporary bridge erected following 1940 war damage. A replacement opened in 2013. The first in 1750 was an unusual wooden geometrical design which appears in a Giovanni Canaletto painting. The second opened in 1783 and was painted by Turner. This is the site of a ford crossed by Julius Caesar in 64. The Walton bank is known as Cowey Sale ('cow way'), and at the back of the low-lying meadow is the Engine River which was probably an earlier Thames channel on the flood plain. The Engine, rather than the Thames, is the former Middlesex–Surrey boundary, and today the boundary between Spelthorne and Elmbridge District Councils.

ALTERNATIVE ROUTE AVOIDING FERRY

Note the final ferry times at Shepperton. See the end of this stage for the alternative waymarked route to Shepperton over Walton Bridge.

Before the next bridge the river divides, giving a choice of navigation between the old channel and the manmade cut under the bridge.

Riverside house near Shepperton

Over a century after **Desborough Cut** was first suggested (and supported by the Grand Old Duke of York living nearby at Weybridge) work began in 1930. The ¾-mile channel, avoiding five tortuous bends, was opened in 1935 by Lord Desborough, Thames Conservancy Board Chairman. Desborough Island, created by the cut, still has the old towpath which gives views of Shepperton Manor and church.

The Thames Path follows the cut ahead. Beyond the second Desborough Island bridge, the Old and New Thames merge and the towpath is soon level with D'Oyly Carte Island.

D'oyly Carte Island was Folly or Silly Eyot until theatre manager Richard D'Oyly Carte decided in about 1890 to build Eyot House on the island, which had become more substantial following dredging. It was to have been the summer annex to the Savoy Hotel, but when a drinks licence was refused the house became D'Oyly Carte's home.

Visitors included William S Gilbert and Sir Arthur Sullivan – willow trees at nearby Shepperton inspired the *Mikado* song 'Tit-willow'. Before the bridge was built visitors called a boat by ringing the bell at the lychgate on the path.

Ahead the towpath crosses the river at the ferry, leaving a riverside path to continue into Weybridge. Ring the bell on the quarter hour to call the ferryboat from the far bank.

Shepperton Ferry reopened in 1986 after a 26-year break. There has been a ferry here since Henry VI's reign. In the 1700s it cost a shilling to take a drove of oxen across for Kingston Market. Between the world wars, when Sid Kingman was ferryman for 22 years, the passenger fare was 1d or 2d for cyclists and the service operated daily 6am–10pm. Today the ferry runs Mon–Fri 8am–6pm; Sat 9am–5pm (BST 6pm); Sun 10am–5pm (BST 6pm). Ring the bell on the quarter hour. Fare £2. Further details 01932 254844.

Old and new towpath fencing near Chertsey

The ferry lands at Ferry Lane on the edge of Shepperton. Turn left along the road to pass Shepperton

Lock. Round the first bend there is Thames Court pub. Opposite is Pharaoh's Island.

The name **Pharaoh's Island** dates from the Battle of the Nile, when the island was given to Lord Nelson. The present 23 properties tend to have Egyptian names such as Ramses, Sphinx and Thebes. Past residents include actor Ian Hendry.

Occasionally it is necessary to walk on the parallel road. When the road moves away from the bank the towpath is on grass with only the occasional Victorian house. Later, where the way narrows, there may be several houseboats. After a kissing gate the towpath is on the edge of Dumpsey Mead as the river bends north. Go through another kissing gate just before Chertsey Bridge beyond the bend.

Alternative Route to Shepperton avoiding Ferry

Cross Walton Bridge to Windmill Green and at once bear half left into Walton Lane. As the road bears sharp left, keep ahead down the side of a wall (left) by a playing field. At Lower Halliford's green go left. Ahead is Peacock House marked by a blue plaque.

The riverside **Peacock House** was bought in 1826 by Thomas Love Peacock, author of the poem *The Genius of the Thames*, for his mother and it became his own home until his death in 1866. His son-in-law novelist George Meredith lived in Vine Cottage across the green.

Cross Walton Lane and bear right on the path past the river viewpoint. Go left into Russell Road to pass the Red Lion and the Ship Hotel. When the narrow pavement ends take the path by the backwater on the left. The path soon rejoins the road. (To reach Shepperton Station continue ahead and go right at the roundabout to walk up the main shopping street.) The Thames Path turns left over a footbridge and right to continue parallel to the road. At

Shepperton Manor

a junction go left up the approach to Shepperton Cricket Club. Just before the cricket ground go left at a gate to find a path which leads to the riverside. Here there is a fine view of Shepperton Manor.

> **Shepperton** means 'shepherds' habitation' and in the Domesday Book belonged to Westminster Abbey. The church was destroyed by flooding during the winter of 1605–6 when the Thames was still tidal here. The present church was built in 1613 with the tower added in the next century. Behind is the Rectory which, when new, in Henry VII's reign, was often visited by the Dutch theologian Desiderius Erasmus, who was a friend of the rector. George Eliot wrote *Scenes from Clerical Life* at Shepperton Manor.

Walk upstream and follow the manor grounds wall to reach Church Road. Go left to pass Church Square (left) and continue into Chertsey Road. Go left down Ferry Lane to Shepperton Lock.

FACILITIES INFORMATION – KINGSTON TO CHERTSEY

Refreshments
Molesey Lock: Café. 8am–6pm; reduced hours in winter.
Sunbury: The Weir (on towpath). 11am–11pm (Sun 12–10.30pm).
   Food all day.
Walton-on-Thames: The Swan. 11am–11pm. (Sun 12–10.30pm.)
   Food 11am–9.30pm; weekends 12.30pm–7.30pm.
Shepperton Lock: Teas and ices in summer.
Shepperton Lock: Thames Court is just upstream from lock. 12–11pm.
   (Sun 12–10.30pm). Food, including children's menu, all day.

Transport
Kingston: National Rail.
Shepperton: National Rail.
Chertsey: National Rail.

Tourist Information
Kingston: The Market House, The Market Place, KT1 1JS (020 8547 5592).

Map
OS Explorer 160 (Windsor) and 161 (London South).

STAGE 5
Chertsey to Staines

Start	Chertsey Bridge
Finish	Staines Bridge
Distance	4 miles (6.4km)

This short section is on the left bank through countryside which has long been a centre for riverside residences and holiday homes. Although only four miles long there are two locks.

CHERTSEY

The first bridge at Chertsey was built in 1410 and maintained by Chertsey Abbey. The present bridge, a little upstream, was completed in 1785. Charles Dickens features the bridge in *Oliver Twist*.

Chertsey, ½ mile from the bridge, was called 'the stillest of towns' by poet Matthew Arnold. The Thames braid from Penton Hook to just above Chertsey Bridge was probably manmade for Chertsey Abbey, which lay behind the parish church. When Henry VI was murdered in the Tower his body (after being exposed at St Paul's) was brought by barge to the abbey, but his tomb became such an object of pilgrimage that after 22 years the coffin was moved further upstream to Windsor. At the Dissolution in 1537 the Benedictine community moved to Bisham, while buildings here were demolished and the stone taken downstream to improve Hampton Court. In 1540 the abbey church's steeple stone went to Weybridge to enlarge a house for the divorced Anne of Cleves. The library and orchard followed on barges. But there was still enough accommodation left in 1548 for Archbishop Cranmer to hold meetings about the first *Book of Common Prayer*. An abbey bell, now in the church, is rung as a curfew at 8pm between Michaelmas and Lady Day. When poet Abraham Cowley died here in 1667 his body was taken by river for burial in Westminster Abbey. In 1776 Chertsey Cricket Club was the first to add the middle stump to the then normal two, due to gardener 'Lumpy' Stevens' bowling skill. The museum in Windsor Street is open Tue-Fri 12.30–4.30pm; Sat 11am–4pm; admission free.

The towpath does not cross Chertsey Bridge to the town side, but continues below and then alongside a road to pass Chertsey Lock. After passing under the M3, the path is separate from the main road, which eventually turns inland at Laleham Ferry.

For 1:25K route map see booklet pages 65–66.

Laleham means 'village by willows'. Laleham House was home of the Lucan family, who remain landowners. The missing earl was golf club president and patron of the church where there is a Lucan Chapel. Churchyard tombs include Lord Lucan of Charge of the Light Brigade fame (east side). Matthew Arnold, buried opposite the small south door, was born at Ferry Lane's Muncaster House where his famous father Thomas ran a school. The ferry, run by a Lucan tenant in Ferry House on the far bank until the late 1970s, provided a short cut to Chertsey.

The towpath is now on a quiet road, but there is more traffic after walled Vicarage Lane. Laleham's church tower can be seen down Blacksmith Lane. Later the towpath again joins a road which, after crossing the Queen Mary Reservoir water intake, leads to Penton Hook Lock.

Here the river takes ½ mile to travel 20 yards. The **lock** opened in 1815, saving the loop, although before this barges often broke through the narrow neck. This was the highest of the locks controlled by the City of London whose arms are seen on the lock cottages.

79

The towpath is now free of cars, but there are residences on both sides as far as Staines. On approaching a bend the path, unusually, does not stay by the water, but hugs the houses before turning north with the Thames. On the far side is Truss's Island.

Truss's Island, restored in 1992 with water again on all sides, is named after the City of London's Navigation Clerk of Works, Charles Truss. The stone, bearing the Corporation shield and the island's name, was placed in the centre in 1804, but has the date 1774, which is the year of his appointment. The City, then responsible for the Thames as far as Staines, had allowed the river to become so obstructed and towpaths so eroded that it was in danger of losing its ancient rights. Truss spent 36 years restoring the river, which saw a huge increase in traffic with the opening of the Thames and Severn Canal.

After ½ mile there is St Peter's Church.

St Peter's Church, opened in 1894 after the arrival of the railway caused Staines to expand south, was financed by Sir Edward Clarke KC who offered to pay for a church if a neighbour bought the gates. The following year he defended Oscar Wilde at his trial. The site was chosen by Lady Clarke, who recalled a church on the banks of Devon's River Dart, and Sir Edward moved swiftly when riverside elms were threatened by a builder. Then the couple lived a little downstream in a house by the towpath with eight acres of garden, but later Sir Edward sold it to Indian cricketer Rangi Singh and built for himself the house next to the church which is now the Vicarage. On Rogation Sunday the St Peter's congregation assembled on the towpath for the blessing of the river.

Ahead is Staines Railway Bridge where the towpath, but not the Thames Path, switches banks.

Staines Railway Bridge, built in 1856 for the Staines–Reading line, was painted with yellow stripes in 1995 to stop swans from flying into it. This point, where the towpath switches banks, was known as Shooting Off, and the early-19th-century cottages immediately upstream of the bridge were called Hook On and Shoot Off, as this was where barges were poled across to the towpath on the right bank while the horses were taken through the town to the bridge. Coming downstream the barge floated over with the current from the far side. The nearby Thames Lodge hotel incorporates the Packhorse where bargees stayed.

Towpath bridge opposite Staines

Beyond the slipway go left through gates by the cottages to follow a riverside path along the back of the former Packhorse. After gardens there is Staines' Market Hall and then a footbridge over the entrance to the River Colne (which rises at Colney Heath near Hatfield). Go under Staines Bridge and at once right to reach steps leading up to the road.

FACILITIES INFORMATION – CHERTSY TO STAINES

Refreshments
Chertsey Bridge: The Boat House. 11am–11pm (Sun 12–10.30pm).
  Food until 9.30pm.

Accommodation
Chertsey Bridge: Camping and Caravanning Club site, Bridge Road
  (01932 562405 before 8pm). Open all year. Non-members welcome.
  Go over bridge from towpath and turn right to find site on riverbank
  opposite lock.
Laleham: Camping Club site, Laleham Park (01932 564149). Apr–Sep.
  Near river to south of village.

Transport
Chertsey: National Rail.
Staines: National Rail.

Map
OS Explorer 160 (Windsor).

STAGE 6
Staines to Windsor

Start	Staines Bridge
Finish	Windsor Bridge
Distance	7½ miles (12km)

Here the towpath passes from Surrey into the Royal County of Berkshire, having first run along the side of Runnymede where Magna Carta was accepted by King John. Opposite Datchet, where the towpath in Windsor Castle grounds is closed to walkers, the Crown Estate has provided new footpaths on the left bank for the Thames Path.

STAINES

When the barons gathered here in 1215 to meet King John on Runnymede they had to ford the river. The first bridge was built seven years later. The present structure, designed by John Rennie (see Stage 2), opened in 1832 a little upstream from the old crossing where the Market Hall now stands. In its predecessor in 1603 Sir Walter Raleigh was found guilty of treason – plague forced the trial out of London. The parish church's tower was built 30 years later, but the landmark is the 1903 Ashley's Brewery, now the Maltings residences. The London Stone, originally just downstream of the bridge but now in the riverside park west of the church, marks the end of the City of London's river jurisdiction (1197–1857). It stands in a playground next to the County Ditch which was the Middlesex–Buckinghamshire boundary. The Lord Mayor made an annual visit to touch the stone with a sword. Staines was the end of the tidal Thames until 1812 when the downstream locks were built. The attractive houses downstream of the bridge and opposite the town date from around 1750.

From Staines cross the bridge and bear right to follow a brick path down to the Thames. Turn left upstream. A high bridge takes the towpath over an inlet opposite Church

For 1:25K route map see booklet pages 63–65.

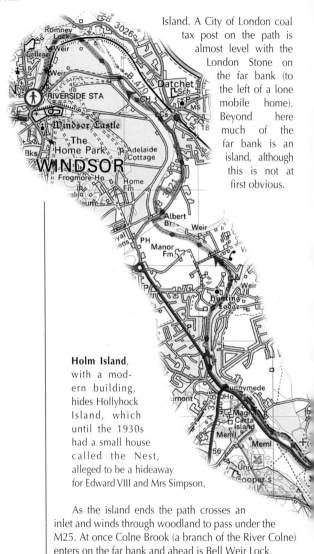

Island. A City of London coal tax post on the path is almost level with the London Stone on the far bank (to the left of a lone mobile home). Beyond here much of the far bank is an island, although this is not at first obvious.

Holm Island, with a modern building, hides Hollyhock Island, which until the 1930s had a small house called the Nest, alleged to be a hideaway for Edward VIII and Mrs Simpson.

As the island ends the path crosses an inlet and winds through woodland to pass under the M25. At once Colne Brook (a branch of the River Colne) enters on the far bank and ahead is Bell Weir Lock.

Bell Weir Lock, dating from 1817, is named after weir keeper and ferryman Charlie Bell who opened the Angler's Rest Hotel here in the 18th century. Its successor, the Runnymede Hotel, has a Charlie Bell's café-bar.

There is a mile of riverside homes broken by a boat-yard. At the end follow the curving bank south with a view over to the wooded grounds of Ankerwycke Priory. After a statue of the Queen on the left the way is between the river and a road running the length of the Runnymede meadow. After Lily Pond Inlet there is a clear view of the Magna Carta Memorial (left).

RUNNYMEDE

King John agreed to Magna Carta somewhere in this field in 1215. The barons' demands were probably approved by the King symbolically kissing Archbishop Langton rather than by the signing of a document which has been called 'the first ground and chief cornerstone of the Common Law of England'. It confirmed the Thames as a highway by declaring that 'all fishweirs shall be entirely removed from the Thames'. The monument on the west side was erected by the American Bar Association. Nearby is the John F Kennedy Memorial, and behind on Cooper's Hill can be seen the Commonwealth Air Forces Memorial. The left-bank Magna Carta Island is claimed by some as the real site of the King's meeting with the barons. The 'island', joined to the far bank, was part of Ankerwycke Priory, and its Benedictine nuns owned the weirs and fisheries between here and Old Windsor.

Honeypot Cottage opposite Old Windsor

At the end of the meadow, where there are two lodges (one is a tearoom), continue through a boatyard. There is a short stretch of quiet towpath before the way is metalled and joins a pavement by a road. The separate towpath is resumed just before the pub.

The Bells of Ouzeley is a 1936 building now run by Harvester Inns. The spelling was 'Ouseley' when it was 'the picturesque inn' described in Jerome K Jerome's *Three Men in a Boat*, written in 1888. The bells are believed to be those of Oxford's Osney Abbey, which in 1538 were being spirited down the river by monks trying to save them from the hands of Henry VIII's agents. When the barges went aground here the bells were hidden in the oozing mud. They have never been found, but the bells of Christ Church Oxford are claimed as those of Osney.

The towpath is in front of a new development and through a former boatyard before a rough surface is resumed. There are houses on both banks and several gardens extend over the towpath. At Old Windsor the path divides.

Old Windsor is where Edward the Confessor had a palace before William the Conqueror moved the royal residence to the present castle site three miles away. Here in 1072 a synod agreed that the Archbishop of Canterbury should take precedence over York. The 13th-century church is unique in having the double dedication to St Peter and St Andrew. Near the churchyard's northeast gate there is the tomb of Mary Robinson, who sat for artists Gainsborough, Romney and Reynolds.

Except to visit the church, go right over the inlet. Soon there is a view of thatched Honeypot Cottage on the far bank.

Honeypot Cottage, built in 1933 with local bricks and thatch, was the home of actress Beryl Reid from 1952 until her death in 1996. She was well known for taking in stray cats and at one time had 13 cats enjoying the round rooms. The square dining room was added by the actress whose ashes were scattered on the riverside garden.

Ahead is Friday Island and Old Windsor Lock.

Friday Island is so called after Man Friday because it is shaped like a footprint. There is a well and a small two-bedroomed thatched cottage almost hidden by willows.

Beyond the lock the path is almost straight along the New Cut, built in 1822 to save a two-bend detour. After the Ham Island bridge the way is a rural path as far as Albert Bridge. To the left is a view of the Copper Horse on Snow Hill in Windsor Great Park.

Albert Bridge and its upstream twin Victoria were designed by Prince Albert in 1851, although both have had their spans rebuilt. Until 1848 it was possible to continue here on the towpath along the side of Home Park attached to Windsor Castle.

Climb the steps up on to Albert Bridge and cross the river. At once take a path on the right which runs down to a kissing gate and under the bridge. Follow a riverside woodland path with a view across the water to Prince Consort Farm buildings. Later the path turns inland to avoid riverside gardens. On reaching a road do not go through the gate, but turn left to walk along the side of another field. At the end turn left along the road to walk into Datchet and rejoin the river at the parish wharf opposite the High Street.

Continue along the road on the pavement and when the houses end turn left through a gate. A path runs down a slope to cross a backwater on to Sumptermead Ait.

DATCHET

Old Bridge House, at the river end of the short High Street, recalls the time when the High Street continued across the river and along a direct tree-lined lane running through Home Park to Windsor. The road, featured in William Shakespeare's *Merry Wives of Windsor*, used a ferry and from 1706 a wooden bridge. This was replaced in 1811 by a half-wooden (on the left Buckinghamshire side) and half-iron (on the Berkshire bank) bridge which lasted until the Victoria and Albert bridges succeeded the Datchet crossing. Much-restored Datchet church has a 13th-century chancel with memorials to Lady Katheryn Barkeley, wife of Elizabeth I's standard bearer, and Christopher Barker, who was the Queen's printer. A milestone opposite records London 20 miles and Windsor 1 mile.

Sumptermead Ait riverside path opened in 1995 as an alternative to the towpath, which remains closed for security reasons. Thanks to a narrow channel

Home Park, Windsor

this is still an island and affords a good view of the Royal Boathouse, where the royal barge (now at the National Maritime Museum) was kept until 1953.

The way is along the stream for a short distance before bearing left to the riverside opposite the Royal Boathouse. Follow the winding path, which crosses a small footbridge, and later a more substantial bridge over the sometimes dry upstream-end of the narrow channel. Go ahead over the grass and up steep steps to Victoria Bridge.

Victoria Bridge gives the first good view of Windsor Castle – as seen by the Queen's guests, arriving here via Datchet on state visits to be welcomed in this northern part of the Home Park before joining a carriage procession to the castle. Also visible is Eton College Chapel.

Cross Victoria Bridge, and at the end of the white railing (right) turn right back to the riverside to rejoin the towpath which runs along the edge of the public section of Home Park. Joining the Thames on the far side, well before Black Pott's railway bridge, is the Maidenhead–Windsor flood-relief channel, opened in 2002 as the Jubilee River.

Black Pott's Bridge, erected in 1849 to carry the Waterloo–Windsor railway line, was designed by Sir Joseph Lock and decorated by Sir William Tite, who was making the nearby station look regal. The crossing was slightly altered in 1892. The origin of the name is uncertain, but this spot has been known as Black Pott's for at least 300 years, when a fishing lodge on the far bank was used by Charles II and Izaac Walton.

The riverbank, rich in wildflowers, has a view of Eton's playing fields beyond an island. During May's Royal Windsor Horse Show the path has stables to the left. At a kissing gate go through a boatyard to a lane which avoids Romney Lock. Soon there is a view of Eton College Chapel. Turn right into fenced Romney Walk, which is by the river and leads to a road. Continue ahead, past a turning to Windsor Riverside station, to Windsor Bridge.

FACILITIES INFORMATION – STAINES TO WINDSOR

Refreshments
Runnymede: Magna Carta Tea Room (in NT lodge). Apr–Sep 10am–5pm;
    Dec–Jan 10am–3.30pm; Feb, Mar, Oct, Nov 10am–4.30pm.

Transport
Staines: National Rail.
Datchet: National Rail.
Windsor: National Rail from Windsor and Eton Riverside or Windsor and
    Eton Central.

Tourist Information
Windsor: Windsor Royal Shopping, Thames Street SL4 1PJ (01753 743900;
    accommodation 01753 743907).

Map
OS Explorer 160 (Windsor).

STAGE 7
Windsor to Maidenhead

Start	Windsor Bridge
Finish	Maidenhead Bridge
Distance	6½ miles (10.5km)

The rural towpath remains on the Buckinghamshire bank, with views of a film set house and Bray village before passing under Maidenhead's Brunel bridge. There are no refreshments on the towpath between Windsor and Maidenhead except in season at Bray Lock.

WINDSOR

Windsor is derived from the Anglo-Saxon 'Wyndesore' meaning 'winding shore', which probably refers to the Thames' twisting course. The castle, begun as a fortress by William the Conqueror, is the Queen's main home and the resting place of many past monarchs, including Henry VI. The exterior is the result of extensive restoration by Sir Jeffry Wyatville for George IV. When a massive fire swept the west end in 1992 water was pumped from the Thames and two years later stone for the restoration came by barge. The only painting destroyed was one which George III had wanted to burn almost 200 years earlier. He also gave Franz de Cleyn's painting *The Last Supper* to the parish church where curate JS Stone wrote the hymn *The Church's One Foundation*. The next door Guildhall, where Prince Charles married Camilla Parker Bowles in 2005, was designed by Sir Christopher Wren, who had to add extra pillars (in fact not quite touching the ceiling) because the council thought it looked unsafe. Almost opposite is a plaque recalling HG Wells' apprenticeship to a draper, portrayed in *Kipps* and *The History of Mr Polly*.

Windsor Bridge is at least an 800-year-old crossing point. Both road and river traffic paid tolls, and in 1736 it was possible to walk over alive for 2d while being carried in a coffin cost 6s 8d. Tolls ended in 1897 after court proceedings, but the toll-keeper's cottage remains as part of Sir Christopher Wren's House Hotel on the Windsor bank. The present 1822 bridge was the first arched bridge on the river. Road traffic was banned in 1970. Until Eton College's 550th anniversary in 1990 boys were not allowed over the bridge into Windsor unless wearing a tie and jacket.

The Thames Path crosses the bridge to Eton. (The tow-path continues briefly on the Windsor side, but the ferry now operates only in late July when a fun fair is on the Eton bank.)

For 1:25K route map see booklet pages 58–63.

Eton College, dominating the village, was inspired by Winchester College and founded by Henry VI. Seventy poor scholars formed the school nucleus and today there are are still 70 'King's Scholars', although most of the school consists of 'Oppidans' paying fees. The chapel was built in the 15th century with the intention of later adding a nave to what is really just the east end choir. Part of the uniform is a black tail coat, worn in mourning for George III. Eton's upstream riverside is known as the Brocas after the Brocas family who gave the land to the college – Sir John de Brocas from Gascony was one of the Black Prince's favourite knights.

Turn left down Brocas Street. Beyond the Waterman's Arms and the Eton College boathouse there is the Brocas meadow, where the towpath joins at the ferry point and main mooring. The way is over grass with a fine view back to the castle. After the wood there is a railway bridge.

Windsor Great Western Bridge, carrying the Great Western Railway (GWR) branch line from Slough, was designed by Brunel and opened in 1849 just months ahead of the London and South Western Railway which was building the Black Pott's Bridge (see Stage 6).

After two footbridges (the first is Lower Bargeman's Bridge) over Cuckoo Weir, the path is on an island only spoilt by the Queen Elizabeth (Windsor relief road) Bridge. On the far bank beyond the bypass is Clewer church on the Mill Stream.

William the Conqueror attended services at **St Andrew's, Clewer**. Buried in the southwest corner

93

of the churchyard (noted for its wild flowers) is Sir Daniel Gooch, GWR's first locomotive engineer, who decided to make Swindon a railway centre. Also buried there is Nanny May (Mary Ann Hull), who looked after Queen Victoria's children as listed on the stone. A now closed convent in nearby Hatch Lane once received prostitutes sent by William Gladstone from London for rehabilitation.

(Clewer church can be reached by going up the path on the upstream side of the bypass bridge, over the bridge and down into the village. Follow the road round to the right.)

Although the main path now cuts the corner, the Thames Path stays with the towpath. The paths are united at a bridge when the towpath leaves the island. There is a view of Eton Wick inland. Behind the trees on the far bank is Windsor Race Course and by the path there is soon a riverside seat at a bank known as Athens.

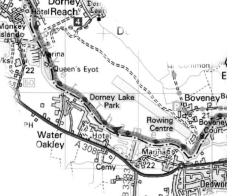

Athens was an Eton College bathing spot where rules required that 'boys who are undressed must either get at once into the water or get behind screens when boats containing ladies come in sight'.

Soon after Boveney Lock there is a last view of Windsor Castle – the upper turret and flagpole can just be seen above the trees. Soon there is Boveney church.

Boveney Church, which has a Norman window, may have been a chapel for nearby Bolney Court, which belonged to Burnham Abbey three miles north. It is now in the care of the Friends of Friendless Churches, which has recently completed work on conserving the 15th-century weatherboarded and timber-framed tower.

After lonely Andrew's Boat House the river bends to give a view of substantial riverside houses at Ruddle's Pool and then Windsor Marina. After a mile the path is level with Oakley Court, which will have been glimpsed earlier.

Oakley Court was built in 1859 as a residence for an Englishman who hoped the Gothic style would make his homesick French wife happy. General de Gaulle is the most famous Frenchman to have visited. In 1950 the house was purchased by Hammer Films

95

Oakley Court

who used it for making *St Trinian's, Half a Sixpence* and *The Rocky Horror Picture Show*. In 1970 the 92-bedroom mansion became a hotel.

Just beyond Queen's Eyot is Bray Marina on the far bank. On the towpath, by an iron cyclists' mile post, an unmarked footpath leads inland, passing through Wallbank Grove (planted 1996) to Dorney Court.

Dorney Court dates from about 1440 and stands on slight high ground to avoid flooding. The house, 'one of the finest Tudor manor houses', has been the home of the Palmer family since 1600, and among the portraits is Sir James Palmer, Governor of the Mortlake Tapestry Works (see Stage 3). Dorney means 'bee island' and honey is sold here. It is also where England's first pineapple may have been grown and given to Charles II who visited here (see Stage 2). The church dates from the Norman period. The house, used as 'Syon' in the film *Lady Jane*, is open on bank holidays in May (and the preceding

Sun) and Sun–Fri in August; 1.30–4pm; admission charge; **www.dorneycourt.co.uk**.

A short distance beyond the Dorney footpath turning, the towpath passes under Summerleaze Bridge.

Summerleaze Bridge opened in 1996 as both a footbridge for public use and a support for a conveyor belt carrying gravel from an excavation for a 1½ mile rowing lake developed by Eton College on the left bank. The bridge is named after the contractor from nearby Maidenhead.

Just before reaching a line of residences at Dorney Reach, where the path is well maintained, there is the beginning of Monkey Island.

Monkey Island probably means 'monks island', as it belonged to Merton Priory on the River Wandle (see Stage 2) which had a house upstream at Amerden Bank. But in 1738 the 3rd Duke of Marlborough decorated the fishing lodge ceiling with monkeys. The island's foundations for building had been strengthened when barges brought rubble from London after the 1666 Great Fire. The lodge has been a hotel since 1840. Edward VII and Queen Alexandra had tea on the lawn with three future sovereigns – George V, Edward VIII and George VI. HG Wells visited several times with Rebecca West, who describes the island in her novel *Return of the Soldier*. The island could only be reached by boat until a footbridge was built from the right bank in 1956. The 'Birmingham Six' spent their first night of freedom here in secret after being released from prison in 1991.

Beyond a gate the way is through a copse and under the M4 bridge (1961) to Amerden Bank. Soon there is Bray Lock and, after Headpile Eyot, a clear view of Bray village on the Berkshire bank. A seat is directly opposite The Waterside Inn.

Dorney Reach towpath

BRAY

Bray is famous for the song *Vicar of Bray*, although which vicar is uncertain. Simon Alwyn adapted to the many changes of the Reformation years, but the song probably refers to Stuart times. The church is early 14th century and among those married there is snooker player Steve Davies. The village is noted for celebrities, including Rolf Harris, who came because it reminded him of his 'river's-edge home in Perth'. Gerald Ratner lived at upstream Somerville (with the American wrap-around balcony). On the Waterside Inn jetty is the warning 'restaurant only', in case anyone thinks it's still the George pub rather than Michel Roux's three-star establishment, opened in 1972. Diners have included the Duke and Duchess of York, who came just two days after announcing their separation. Journalist John MacCarthy first met friend and campaigner Jill Morrell while on an outing to the inn – the group made alternative arrangements when they saw the expensive menu. The inn is next to Ferry Lane, but a ferry no longer runs across to the seat.

After reaching a house the path is gravelled and then metalled to pass under Maidenhead Railway Bridge.

Maidenhead Railway Bridge, completed by Brunel in 1839, carries the Paddington–Bristol railway line and appears in Turner's 1844 painting *Rain, Steam and Speed on the GWR*. These are the largest and flattest brick arches ever built and many thought they would collapse under the first train. A shout or whistle from below will echo. The bridge, widened in 1893, partly rests on Guards Club Island – the club was on the far bank.

Continue ahead along the road, and beyond gates bear left on a path running back to the waterside. Pass a boatyard and new houses at Taplow Quay to go under Maidenhead Bridge. At once bear right to a gate leading to Mill Lane. To the left is Skindles. Go right to the main road and right again over the bridge to pass from Taplow to Maidenhead.

FACILITIES INFORMATION – WINDSOR TO MAIDENHEAD

Refreshments
Windsor has many cafés and pubs.

Transport
Windsor: National Rail to Windsor and Eton Riverside or Windsor and
   Eton Central.
Maidenhead: National Rail.

Tourist Information
Windsor: Windsor Royal Shopping, Thames Street SL4 1PJ (01753 743900;
   accomodation 01753 743907).

Map
OS Explorer 160 (Windsor) and 172 (Chiltern Hills East).

STAGE 8
Maidenhead to Marlow

Start	Maidenhead Bridge
Finish	Marlow Bridge
Distance	7 miles (11.2km)

This is one of the very attractive stretches of the river and rich in heritage. After the most famous lock there is Cliveden Reach and a diversion from the riverbank to pass through Cookham, made famous by artist Stanley Spencer. The way is then along the edge of rare marshland before turning a corner into the attractive Chiltern town of Marlow.

There has been a **bridge** here on the main London road, linking Maidenhead (right bank) with Taplow, since the mid 13th century when a hermit collected tolls. It was over a much-repaired wooden bridge that William of Orange passed in 1688 to accept the crown in London. The present bridge, completed in 1777, is similar to Swinford Bridge, also designed by Sir Robert Taylor. The latter retains its tolls, but charges ceased here in 1903 after an enquiry exposed misuse of revenues. Skindles, on the left upstream bank, was the Orkney Arms until 1833, when William Skindle turned it from a coaching inn into a fashionable hotel.

For 1:25K route map see booklet pages 55–58.

On the Maidenhead side go upstream through a public garden to join Ray Mead Road. Beyond a riverside building go right to reach Chandler's Quay where the path crosses Clapper's Stream. Rejoin the road and soon after Riverside Gardens there is Boulter's Lock.

Boulter's Lock, the river's longest and deepest, was once the busiest. It is still the most famous, thanks to EJ Gregory's 1898 painting *Boulter's Lock – Sunday Afternoon*, showing the lock packed with small pleasure craft when ex-naval cutlass instructor WH Turner was lock keeper. The mill stream runs between Boulter's Island and Ray Mill Island which is reached by a bridge. The Boulter's Inn is the former flour mill, built in 1726.

The first miller in 1348 was called Ray and in 1773 Richard Ray became lock keeper. 'Boulter', derived from 'bolter' meaning 'miller', gave its name to the lock from 1847. Broadcaster Richard Dimbleby lived on the northern tip of Boulter's Island and was known to shout at speeding boats to slow down (see below).

After 100 yards the road leaves the river and the path continues beyond a TC gate.

This is the first of the blue-grey **Thames Conservancy Gateways** on the towpath. Each is numbered, with the lowest being near Lechlade, although number 1 has gone. New gates erected by the Environment Agency successor are dark wood.

Across the water, just before the weir steam, is the grey wooden home of Richard Dimbleby. On the left there is the restored former Maidenhead Court Boathouse, but the most impressive of the substantial Victorian buildings is the last – Islet Park House – where White Brook serves as an approach to its boathouse. After the path has run inside a line of trees there are fields inland, and after ½ mile the path is level with Spring Cottage in the Cliveden grounds.

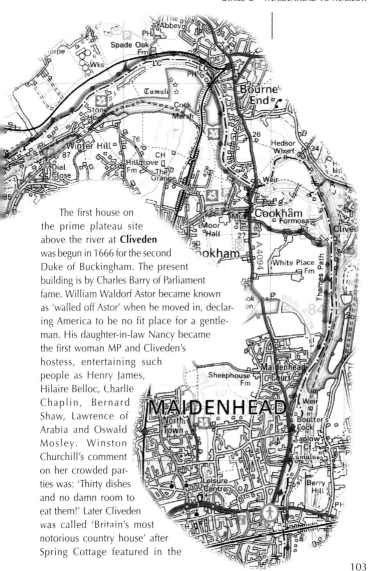

The first house on the prime plateau site above the river at **Cliveden** was begun in 1666 for the second Duke of Buckingham. The present building is by Charles Barry of Parliament fame. William Waldorf Astor became known as 'walled off Astor' when he moved in, declaring America to be no fit place for a gentleman. His daughter-in-law Nancy became the first woman MP and Cliveden's hostess, entertaining such people as Henry James, Hilaire Belloc, Charlle Chaplin, Bernard Shaw, Lawrence of Arabia and Oswald Mosley. Winston Churchill's comment on her crowded parties was: 'Thirty dishes and no damn room to eat them!' Later Cliveden was called 'Britain's most notorious country house' after Spring Cottage featured in the

An original Thames Conservancy, or TC, towpath gate

Profumo affair. When told the mansion was to become a hotel, Harold Macmillan commented: 'My dear boy, it always has been.' It was Lady Penelope's residence in the *Thunderbirds* film.

The towpath switches bank at the former My Lady Ferry.

My Lady Ferry, the last operated by Thames Conservancy, ran until 1956. The towing horses had to be moved to the left bank for just under ½ mile before returning to the right bank to go up Cookham Lock Cut on its left side. The operation between here and Cookham Bridge involved three ferries. Ferry Cottage opposite is rented out as a holiday home by the National Trust, with the short stretch of towpath outside still a public footpath.

The Thames Path now turns inland through a wood and later is parallel to a drive. Beyond a stile bear half left

104

on a path which curves round to join Mill Lane. At the
end turn right to walk into the centre of Cookham village.

COOKHAM

The church, scene of many weddings including actress Susan George's in
1984, has a 12th-century nave. The churchyard features in Stanley Spencer's
painting *The Resurrection* – the artist's grave is to left of the path at a point
where the view and painting can be compared. He was born at Fernlea
in the High Street near the Methodist church, which is now the Stanley
Spencer Gallery – England's only gallery devoted to a 20th-century artist
(1891–1959). *Christ Preaching at Cookham Regatta* is set at the back of the
Ferry Inn, and in *The Crucifixion* the tormentors are said to be based on
local faces. He said: 'You can't walk by the river at Cliveden Reach and not
believe in God.' Cookham Bridge, which appears in his *Swan Upping*, was
built in 1867 to replace the original of 1840. The tollhouse, which operated
until 1947, is on the far bank. Lullebrook Manor in Ferry Lane is said to
be the inspiration for 'Toad Hall' in *The Wind in the Willows* – its author
Kenneth Grahame lived nearby when the manor's owner was the first person
in the village to have a motor car.

Continue past the High Street (left) and Odney
Lane (right) to go left by timber-framed cottages into the
churchyard. Take the main path to the left of the church
to find the river beyond a narrow kissing gate. The walk
continues to the left upstream, past the sailing club
and along the edge of Cock Marsh opposite the mainly
Edwardian houses of Bourne End.

Cock Marsh is one of the few remaining examples
of lowland marsh and an exceptionally good site
for seeing redshank, lapwing and wading birds. The
burial mounds west of the railway are evidence of
Bronze Age occupation.

Beyond the kissing gate into the National Trust area
keep to the right of the belt of trees. Go through a gate to
pass under the railway bridge.

Bourne End Railway Bridge succeeded an 1857 wooden structure carrying a single track. The present iron-and-steel bridge was opened in 1894 with provision for a second track. The line no longer runs to High Wycombe but carries just the single track for the Maidenhead–Marlow shuttle. The footbridge was attached in 1993 for the Thames Path to save a long walk over Winter Hill. Before this there was an electric bell on a Bourne End bank tree for those wanting to be rowed over to the Bounty pub on the Cock Marsh side.

A short distance ahead is the Bounty pub, but the Thames Path turns left up the steps and across the bridge. Once on the Bourne End side turn left, (but go right and left to reach Bourne End Station). The footpath runs near the river and through Bourne End Marina. After becoming briefly enclosed again, the path passes through the Upper Thames Sailing Club grounds before running behind more riverside gardens to a kissing gate at Spade Oak Ferry.

Spade Oak Ferry, which ceased running in 1962, is where the towpath crosses the river. Ferry Cottage can be seen opposite with Winter Hill at the back of Cock Marsh.

The way ahead is through a series of towpath gates and past two islands. Later there is a view of an impressive castellated house. The river turns west below Quarry Wood to pass Longridge Scout Boating Centre on the far bank and flow under Marlow bypass.

Marlow Bypass, completed in 1972, was the Thames walkers' crossing before the Bourne End footbridge opened. The bridge spans Sherriff Island, which was purchased for the Scout Boating Centre in 1976 with a legacy from playwright RC Sherriff, whose royalties now benefit scouts here. Quarry Wood may be the 'wild wood' in *The Wind in the Willows*.

Beyond a line of houses there is a field. Only navigation can reach the lock, so the towpath bears inland to a road. Turn left at Mill Road to follow an S-bend past Marlow Mill (left) and the Mill House (right).

Marlow Mill in the early 19th century embraced three mills, including one producing England's first brass thimbles which were taken upstream to a warehouse on a City of London wharf. Mill House was home of author Sir Evelyn Wrench, who founded the English Speaking Union and Royal Overseas League.

There is a view of Marlow's weir, suspension bridge and church before the road turns inland. Follow the wall and go left along Seven Corner Alley which leads to St Peter Street and the Two Brewers.

The Two Brewers was frequented by Jerome K Jerome who is said to have worked on part of *Three Men in a Boat* here, although most was written in a Chelsea flat. The Swan Uppers visit the pub every summer during their progress upstream checking on swans. Until recently the sign showed Thomas Wethered, founder of Marlow's brewery, on one side and Samuel Whitbread, who bought Wethered's, on the other. Seven Corner Alley, alongside the pub, was used by towing horses being led between the lock and Marlow Bridge, which until 1832 was at the end of St Peter Street. Until 1773 there was also a winch at the end of the road for hauling barges over a flash lock on the site of the weir.

Cross St Peter Street to go down a second alley by the Old Malt House opposite the Two Brewers to reach Marlow's churchyard and the Causeway.

FACILITIES INFORMATION – MAIDENHEAD TO MARLOW

Refreshments
Maidenhead: Jenner's tea hut in Riverside Gardens is open most days.
Cookham: The Ferry Inn by bridge. 11am–11pm.
Cookham: Teapot Tea Shop, 1–2 Clieve Cottages, High Street. 10am–5pm.
Cock Marsh: The Bounty pub. Apr–Sept 12–11pm. Food 12–8pm. Oct–Mar
    Sat & Sun 12 to dusk. Food until 5pm or earlier if dark.

Accommodation
Maidenhead Bridge (Taplow side): Bridge Cottage Guest House, Bath Road,
    SL6 0AR (01628 626805).

Transport
Maidenhead: National Rail. Cookham: National Rail.
Marlow: National Rail.

Tourist Information
Maidenhead: The Library, St Ives Road, SL6 1QU (01628 796502).

Map
OS Explorer 172 (Chiltern Hills East).

STAGE 9

Marlow to Henley

Start	Marlow Bridge
Finish	Henley Bridge
Distance	8½ miles (13.6km)

Only thanks to a new bridge is it possible to again follow the river all the way from Marlow to Henley. On this stretch the path passes through three counties and alongside three ancient monastic sites before reaching the straight rowing course leading to Henley Bridge.

MARLOW

The 1835 All Saints replaced the 12th-century church undermined by centuries of flooding. In the porch is a memorial (the oldest erected at public expense) to Sir Miles Hobart who started the House of Commons custom of slamming the door in Black Rod's face – Hobart's death caused by bolting horses on Holborn Hill is depicted. Artist EJ Gregory, who lived at 100 High Street, is buried in the churchyard. Next to the partly 14th-century Old Parsonage in St Peter's Street is St Peter's, by Augustus Pugin, which has St James the Great's hand (not displayed). Poet Percy Shelley, who kept a skiff for Thames expeditions, lived at Albion House (marked by plaque) in West Street in 1817, writing *The Revolt of Islam* while his wife Mary produced *Frankenstein*. Earlier they had lived with Thomas Love Peacock at number 67 (now a car park). A century on TS Eliot lived at number 31 (an old post office). The present bridge, based on Hammersmith Bridge, opened in 1832. The mansion in Higginson Park just upstream of the bridge was built in the 1760s for mental illness specialist Dr William Battie – hence the term 'batty'. The Compleat Angler hotel on the Berkshire bank stands on the spot where Izaak Walton is supposed to have written *The Compleat Angler* in 1653.

Walk to the bridge and keep right to follow a path down the side to the towpath. Beyond the town mooring at Higginson Park there is a view over the water to Bisham church and the next-door abbey.

For 1:25K route map see booklet pages 52–55.

Bisham Church, with its landmark Norman tower, has been called 'a jewel on the riverside'. Floodwater can reach the pulpit. Buried in a magnificent chapel is diplomat Sir Philip Hoby, whose body was brought by river from his Blackfriars house (see Stage 2) in 1588. It was on this reach that Shelley spent

much time floating in a skiff writing *The Revolt of Islam*, which features a river and a boat.

Bisham Abbey is the National Sports Centre and the England football team headquarters. The first building was occupied by the Knights Templars in 1139, but after their suppression in 1307 an Augustinian priory was established. Warwick the King-maker was buried here in 1471 after the Battle of Barnet. Although closed by Henry VIII in 1536, the monastery soon reopened as an abbey for Benedictines displaced from Chertsey (see Stage 5) who were to pray for the late Queen Jane (Seymour). But in the following year it too was dissolved by the King who later gave the property to his second queen, Anne of Cleves, as a consolation for her divorce. She did a swap with Philip Hoby for his house in Kent. The future Elizabeth I spent three years here and returned as Queen in 1597. Elizabeth II visited in her 2002 jubilee year.

The towpath, having passed through a couple of TC gateways, comes level with Temple Mill Island.

Temple Mill Island takes its name from the Templars who ran the mill. In 1710 this was a copper foundry which was enlarged when the open- ing of the Thames

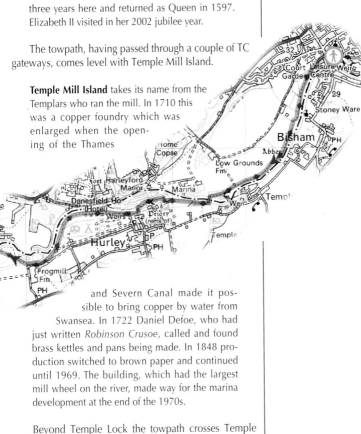

and Severn Canal made it pos- sible to bring copper by water from Swansea. In 1722 Daniel Defoe, who had just written *Robinson Crusoe*, called and found brass kettles and pans being made. In 1848 pro- duction switched to brown paper and continued until 1969. The building, which had the largest mill wheel on the river, made way for the marina development at the end of the 1970s.

Beyond Temple Lock the towpath crosses Temple Bridge to the Berkshire bank.

Temple Bridge, a 150ft span, is Britain's longest hardwood footbridge, which in 1989 replaced a ferry that had not operated since 1953.

Continue upstream under a line of trees with a view half right of Harleyford Manor.

111

Temple Bridge

Harleyford Manor, another house (now offices) said to be the inspiration for Kenneth Grahame's 'Toad Hall', was built in 1755 by architect Sir Robert Taylor for Sir Robert Clayton.

The towpath crosses a high bridge on to Hurley's Lock Island. On returning to the mainland after Hurley Lock keep ahead only to visit Hurley village.

Hurley is hidden from the towpath. The church was the chapel of a Benedictine priory consecrated in 1086 by St Osmund. Edward the Confessor's wife is buried in an unmarked grave. The refectory is now a private house, but the guest house continues in business as Ye Olde Bell. Lady Place stands on the site of a building where James II's overthrow was planned by Protestants. Later a grateful William of Orange paid a visit. Elizabeth II embarked here for Runnymede in 1964. Wooden boats are built here by Peter Freebody whose family has worked on the river since at least the

13th century. His ancestor John was working as a bargeman on the same riverside site in 1642.

The Thames Path continues upstream, over the high bridge at a boatyard inlet (where the old boathouse was damaged by fire) and through a small gate into a large meadow. The far bank is a high cliff. The river bends south and after a second kissing gate it is possible to look back and see Danesfield on top of the cliff.

Danesfield takes it name from the Danes who came upstream and built a strategic fortification. The mansion, faced with local stone and designed by Romaine Walker, was completed in 1901 for Robert Hudson of Hudson's Soap fame. After being an RAF station (1941–77) it opened as a hotel in 1991. The previous house on the site was home of Charles Scott-Murray who added a chapel (demolished) by Pugin housing the St James' hand (see page 109).

The path joins a track in front of Frogmill's riverside homes. At a third gate, by Water's Edge, bear half right to stay by the water as the main path veers away. The towpath runs past islands. Beyond here the Thames Path keeps ahead through a gate to cut a corner and run directly to Medmenham Ferry, but for a good view of Medmenham Abbey stay on the towpath.

Medmenham Abbey was a Cistercian foundation, begun in 1201 and closed in 1536 when the community comprised of only the abbot and one monk. There is a remaining 13th-century pillar, but the attractive ruins are largely contrived. The building is best known for Sir Francis Dashwood's notorious Hell Fire Club, which met there between 1750 and 1774. Members, who included John Wilkes and Lord Sandwich, were known as 'Franciscans of Medmenham' after their host was alleged to have performed obscene parodies of religious rites. The ferry was used by Charles II, Edward VII and

Medmenham Abbey

George V, who was accompanied by Queen Mary. Although an historic 1899 court ruling confirmed the public's right to use this ferry it has ceased operation.

At the ferry point the towpath switches banks, leaving the Thames Path to continue on the right bank through a kissing gate. There are three ditches crossed by footbridges. Beyond the third one bear half left across a field to a gap in the middle of the far side. Turn right along a track which runs uphill past a pink cottage. Where the way becomes a footpath keep ahead for a few yards and go through a gate on the right. Keep ahead to a gate leading to a second field. Pass through kissing gates flanking the vista between Culham Court and the Thames below.

Culham Court was built in 1770, but its architect is unknown. When George III stayed in 1804 fresh breakfast rolls wrapped in warm flannels were rushed down from London by horse relay. In the early 20th century the house was home of Lady Barber, who founded Birmingham's Barber Institute of Fine Arts just before her death in 1932, and after the Second World War the occupant was banker and arts patron Michael Behrens.

Keep along the top of a ridge to reach a gate at the far end of the meadow. Keep forward to follow the estate road ahead downhill to Aston. Turn right to reach the Flower Pot.

The Flower Pot advertised 'boatman always in attendance' in 1893, but the ferry bringing the tow-path back to this side has ceased to run. However, still painted on the inn's outside wall is 'good accommodation for fishing and boating parties'. There are old Thames pictures and fish on the walls. Chickens run around the garden.

Continue past the inn (left) down Ferry Lane to join the towpath which returns to this bank at the end of the road. Soon there is a view of Hambleden Mill and Lock.

Hambleden Mill was working until 1955, having been in existence since the 13th century. A 300-yard narrow public footpath runs across the weir from the lock to the mill.

The Thames Path stays on the right bank beyond the lock. After a short distance the grass gives way to a hard surface which improves as it continues all the way to Henley. Soon there is a view of a white mansion, Greenlands, on the far bank below the beech woods on the Chiltern hillsides.

Greenlands, built in 1853, was the home of book-seller WH Smith. When first lord of the Admiralty he was lampooned in Gilbert and Sullivan's *HMS Pinafore* as 'ruler of the queen's navee'. Since 1946 the house has been occupied by Henley Business School. In the Civil War the original 1604 build-ing was bombarded from across the water by Cromwellian forces flushing out Royalists.

The towpath turns south to approach the Henley Regatta course which runs from Temple Island to Henley Bridge.

Temple Island near Henley

Temple Island, sometimes called Regatta Island and now owned by Henley Royal Regatta, once belonged to Fawley Court just upstream on the far bank. The 'temple', intended as a focus for a vista from the mansion, is a fishing lodge designed in 1771 by James Wyatt who added frescoes inside.

After 400 yards the towpath passes through an old TC gateway at Remenham which faces Fawley Court.

Remenham is a hamlet with a church serving a huge parish. St Nicholas's tower dates from 1836, and the main building restored in 1870 has an apse built on the line of the Norman predecessor. Actress Jenny Agutter was married here. Buried in the churchyard is Caled Gould, who died in 1836 aged 92 having been Hambleden lock keeper since 1777. Descendant Bryan Gould had a London Thames-side home when he was an MP.

    Fawley Court on the left bank has been known as 'Poland-on-Thames' since 1953, when the house became a school for the sons of exiled Poles. The rebuilding in the 1680s followed the sacking of the house by Royalists in the Civil War. Visitors have included William III and William IV.

Immediately after a high bridge the towpath passess the first white riverside house called Barn Elms.

Barn Elms was home of actress Gladys Cooper from the early fifties until her death here in 1971. She walked the towpath daily even in her last year.

Just before Henley Bridge there is the Leander Club.

The Leander Club, founded in 1818, is Britain's oldest rowing club. Members include Olympic

Bisham Abbey

medallists. The building was erected in 1897 – exactly a century before women were admitted as members.

Cross Henley Bridge to leave Berkshire and enter Henley on the Oxfordshire bank.

FACILITIES INFORMATION – MARLOW TO HENLEY

Refreshments
Marlow: Burger's, corner of the Causeway and Station Road. Celebrated baker's taken over by Swiss Burger family in 1942 and now producing 32 kinds of chocolate. Tearoom open Mon–Sat 8.30am–5.30pm; Sun 11m–5pm.
Marlow: Bonny's, 59 High Street. Teas until 5pm daily.
Aston: The Flower Pot. Mon–Fri 11am–4pm and 6–11pm (weekends all day.) Food 12–2.30pm and 6.30–9pm except Sun evening.

Accommodation
Marlow: 18 Rookery Court, SL7 3HR (01628 486451).
Marlow: 8 Firview Close, SL7 1SZ (01628 485735)
Marlow: 10 Lock Road, SL7 1QP (01628 473875).
Hurley: Lock Island camping site (01628 824334). Apr–Sep.
Aston: The Flower Pot. See above (01491 574721).

Transport
Marlow: National Rail.
Henley: National Rail.

Tourist Information
Marlow: Library, Institute Road, SL7 1BL (01628 483597).

Map
OS Explorer 171 (Chiltern Hills West) and 172 (Chiltern Hills East).

STAGE 10
Henley to Reading

Start	Henley Bridge
Finish	Reading Bridge
Distance	9 miles (14.5km)

The exit from Henley is as attractive as the entry from the north. At Marsh Lock the towpath runs out on a long wooden horse bridge into the middle of the river before passing Happy Valley. After Shiplake, where the water is briefly lost behind riverside residences, the Thames is a green corridor into Reading by way of attractive Sonning.

HENLEY-ON-THAMES

Henley-on-Thames church, first recorded in 1204, was served by upstream Dorchester monks. The present building dates from about 1400, like next-door Chantry House. The church tower, built about 1550, contains a monument to William Hayward who, just before his death in 1782, designed Henley Bridge, described by Horace Walpole as 'the most beautiful in the world after the Ponti di Triniti at Florence'. Henley's earlier 14th-century bridge had buildings including a chapel. Outside the church's northwest door is the tomb of Richard Jennings who headed the St Paul's Cathedral building team. The Sacred Heart Church, in Vicarage Road towards the south of the town, incorporates the east end of downstream Danesfield's chapel. The Angel is 18th-century and now looks across the water not at the Carpenters Arms but Terry Farrell's Henley Royal Regatta HQ. The Regatta, founded in 1839, is held during the first week in July. The first University Boat Race was rowed here in 1829. Charles I stayed twice at the Red Lion, and in Hart Street is Speaker's House, birthplace of Speaker Lenthall, who was confronted in the chamber by the King. In John Mortimer's *Paradise Postponed* this is Hartscombe town, but with the closure of Brakspeare's brewery the distinctive aroma has gone from the waterfront. The River and Rowing Museum building, designed by David Chipperfield and inspired by Oxfordshire barns and opened in 1998 on Mill Marsh Meadows, is open daily.

For 1:25K route
map see booklet
pages 47–51.

From the bridge turn upstream behind the Angel. At Hobbs and Sons the traffic leaves the towpath, which soon runs past Mill Marsh Meadows where the River and Rowing Museum is behind the trees. Just beyond the Old House turn left on to a long wooden bridge running out to Marsh Lock.

The reason for the long wooden **horse bridge** across the weir stream to the lock and back is that there was a mill, used for a brass foundry, in the way. A flour mill was on the Berkshire bank, which is still known as Mill Bank.

Soon after returning to the left bank there is a gate on the Henley boundary. The way is now alongside a meadow with a view soon across the water to a rustic bridge over the end of Happy Valley.

The **bridge** carrying the Henley–Wargrave road was built in 1763 with stone from Reading Abbey. The valley beyond is in the grounds of Park Place, seat of Frederick, Prince of Wales, in the 18th century.

Along this reach are 1908 Conservancy markers to indicate a once 14ft-wide towpath – which shows how much erosion has occurred. The river bends at the former Bolney Ferry, just

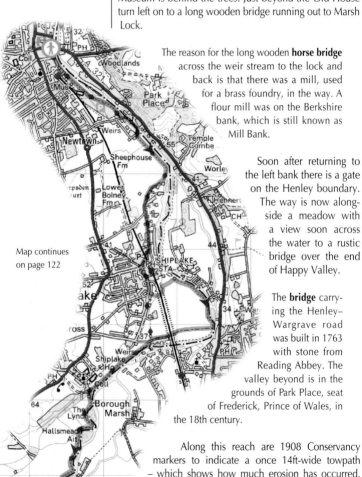

Map continues
on page 122

downstream of Ferry Ayot, where the towpath crosses the river. Continue on the Thames Path as it heads half right inland to a footbridge. The way is briefly enclosed. Cross a track to find the path continuing to the left of a gateway. Soon there is Thames-Side Court's garden and railway (left).

Henley Bridge and church

Happy Valley

Thames-Side Court, built in 1914, is the home of millionaire polo enthusiast Urs Schwarzenbach, who in the early 1990s landscaped the eight-acre garden and added the extensive narrow-gauge railway running alongside the river.

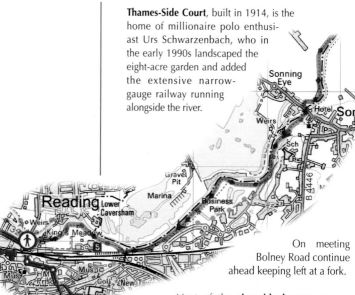

On meeting Bolney Road continue ahead keeping left at a fork.

Most of the **riverside houses** are Edwardian and one has a narrow-gauge railway (narrower than Thames-Side, see above). Past riverside residents here have included playwright Terence Rattigan and fashion designer Norman Hartnell.

On reaching (new) Rivermead House (right) go half right up a narrow footpath which crosses a drive and leads to a kissing gate near the railway line. Do not cross the line but go left to reach the road. Go over the level crossing to Shiplake Station.

Shiplake is a scattered village with the riverside church not reached for two miles. Author George Orwell lived as a child at Roselawn (top of station Road on corner of Quarry Lane).

Keep ahead up Station Road and past The Baskerville to the crossroads. Turn left along Mill Road to the

junction with New Road. Here go left down a lane by Virginia Cottage.

Beyond the white weatherboarded building (right) and Brookfield (left) keep forward. After crossing two bridges the way bears left with a view over a field before veering half left into trees. Go under the low railway bridge to a kissing gate.

Keep ahead over a field and on reaching ditch keep it to the left to reach a gated bridge. Continue forward across a second field towards a gate some yards to the left of a stile. Until the last moment the river is unseen but the gate leads to the towpath and a seat. Opposite is Henley Sailing Club.

Turn right upstream on the fenced path. Soon there is a boatyard on the far bank and moorings along the towpath. The path briefly loses its clear river view to trees before reaching Wargrave Ferry opposite the St George & Dragon.

Here, until waymarking indicates otherwise, leave the towpath by going left through a kissing gate. Follow the field fence (right) to reach a farm gate at the far end.

Narrow-gauge railway station at Thames-Side Court

Go under the railway to a lane passing a line of riverside houses. The last is Mill House. Follow its high wall (left) along a path to Shiplake Lock.

Shiplake Lock island has been a summer campsite since the 1890s with two families being regulars during the next century.

Before the lock go right through a kissing gate to follow the towpath alongside a meadow. There is a gate and a redundant TC stile before the way becomes enclosed at a kissing gate below Shiplake House. At a lawn a path runs behind sheds up to Shiplake Church.

The south aisle of **Shiplake Church** dates from 1140. The font is a copy of the one in Iffley church (see Stage 16).

The towpath continues over the high bridge. Look back to see Shiplake church on the hill before the way double bends to run through a wood opposite two islands. The path is alongside a series of fields until reaching a willow and poplar wood near Sonning. Just before the bridge there is an attractive redundant gateway (right) to the French Horn Hotel inland at Sonning Eye. Cross to Sonning Island and turn left over the road bridge, passing from Oxfordshire to Berkshire as indicated on the stone in the middle (right) to reach Sonning.

SONNING

Sonning is pronounced 'sunning', which was still the spelling in the late 18th century. The church was founded in Saxon times with the present building dating from 1180. It had a St Sarik Chapel, which was a place of pilgrimage for the mentally ill, and the Bull next to the churchyard was the pilgrim lodging. The Bishop of Salisbury had a house on high ground southwest of the church from 1075. Bishop Roger set out from here by barge in 1135 for Henry I's funeral at Reading. In 1574 the estate was sold to Elizabeth I, who visited twice. Deanery Garden, an arts and crafts style house designed

Sonning post office and tea-room

by Edwin Lutyens and completed in 1902 for *Country Life* editor Edward Hudson, has grounds laid out by Gertrude Jekyll, incorporating the Dean of Salisbury's walled garden. The bishop maintained a wooden bridge which was succeeded by the present river crossing in 1772. William Morris dined at the White Hart (now the Great House Hotel) during his journey upstream in 1880. The island's mill, which supplied Huntley and Palmers at Reading, was working until 1969, and until 1950 had its own barge fleet to bring wheat from London Docks.

From the bridge go right along the hard surface tow-path, which has a brief view of 17th-century Mill House (right), to Sonning Lock. The towpath continues alongside trees with occasional views over to lakes behind the far bank. Later the path runs out on to a large meadow which is cut once a year. Stay on the wide grass path by the river, and halfway along cross a bridge over a narrow water chan-nel dug for a now demolished power station. Shortly after the Reading Town Regatta Boathouse the now metalled path swings round to the Kennet and Avon Canal entrance. Cross the canal mouth by using Horseshoe Bridge.

> **Horseshoe Bridge**, replacing a ferry and attached to Brunel's 1839 Great Western Railway bridge, dates from 1892, and has high sides to prevent the towing horses from being frightened at the high crossing. The canal runs to Newbury and Bath.

On the far side the path enters Reading. In the wood-land there is a gateway to Tesco (supermarket and café) opposite a mooring where customers can arrive by water. On entering King's Meadow keep by the water to stay on the towpath, although the metalled path also leads to Caversham Lock – in 1996 the first to have a full-time woman lock keeper for over a century. Beyond is Reading Bridge. To reach Reading Station turn left along the far side of the Bridge and right at the road.

FACILITIES INFORMATION – HENLEY TO READING

Refreshments
Henley has many cafés and pubs.
Shiplake (station end): The Baskerville, Station Road. Open all day.
Sonning: The Bull, next to the churchyard. 10am–11pm (Sun 10am–10.30pm).
Reading: Tesco café, on towpath between Horseshoe Bridge and King's Meadow.

Accommodation
Henley: Alushta Bed and Breakfast, 23 Queen Street RG9 1AR (01491 636041).
Henley: Lenwade, 3 Western Road, RG9 1JL (01491 573468,
   www.lenwade.com).
Henley: Swiss Farm campsite (01491 573419). Mar–Oct. Take right fork at
   end of Bell Street.
Shiplake: The Baskerville, Station Road, RG9 3NY (0118 940 3332,
   www.thebaskerville.com). Near station.

Transport
Henley: National Rail.
Shiplake: National Rail.
Reading: National Rail.

Tourist Information
Henley: Town Hall, Market Place, RG9 2AQ (01491 578034).

Map
OS Explorer 171 (Chiltern Hills West).

STAGE 11
Reading to Pangbourne

Start	Reading Bridge
Finish	Whitchurch Bridge
Distance	7 miles (11.2km)

Reading may have expanded in the last half of the 20th century, but the river still provides a pleasant route through the conurbation of Reading, Caversham, Tilehurst and Purley. Pangbourne is reached after a pleasant meadow walk with views of two historic mansions.

For 1:25K route map see booklet pages 44–47.

From Reading Bridge go upstream past Fry's Island.

Fry's Island, home of the only bowls club in Britain reached by ferry, is known locally as De Montfort Island after a duel fought there in 1163 between Robert de Montfort and Henry Earl of Essex in the presence of Henry II. De Montfort had accused Essex of dropping the royal standard during a battle with the Welsh, but Essex denied the charge. In the duel,

READING

Reading received its royal charter in 1253, but the abbey was founded in 1121 when stone from France was brought up the Thames and unloaded on the Kennet. Later pilgrims came to see the hand of St James the Great. Alongside the ruins is a new church built partly with abbey stones. The Benedictine monastery's closure and partial destruction in 1539 has left Henry I's body buried somewhere under a playground. St Laurence's, part of the abbey precinct, remains intact, and here the future Archbishop Laud, son of a Reading draper, was baptised in 1573. Later Jane Austen went to school in the surviving abbey gateway. In the ruined chapter house are the words and music of the oldest recorded English song *Sumer is icumen in*. The Lady Chapel site is now occupied by the gaol where Oscar Wilde was imprisoned in 1895. Three famous businesses were founded here: Sutton, born in the year of Waterloo, turned his father's corn merchant's into Sutton Seeds; Thomas Huntley, who made biscuits for travellers, teamed up with George Palmer to form Huntley and Palmer's (export biscuits went by barge to London Docks), and hatter Austin Reed opened the first shop in 1900. The railway's arrival had a huge effect on the town, which soon became Berkshire's county capital, replacing Abingdon. Reading Museum (open Tue–Sat 10am–4pm; Sun 11–4pm; admission free) has a replica of the Bayeux Tapestry and displays on the abbey.

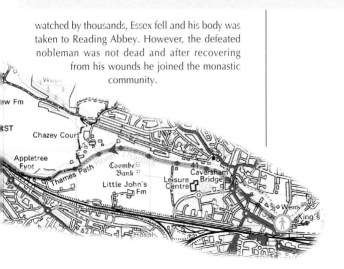

watched by thousands, Essex fell and his body was taken to Reading Abbey. However, the defeated nobleman was not dead and after recovering from his wounds he joined the monastic community.

A house at Caversham

Ahead there is a view of Caversham's St Peter's Church on a hill. Just past the Riverside pub (on a boatyard site) is Caversham Bridge.

Caversham Bridge is the third here. The first was built about 1219 by Reading Abbey to improve the road to Oxford. On the downstream side, near the Caversham bank, there was St Anne's Chapel, where relics included the dagger used to murder Henry VI. Stone from this chapel is now incorporated into Our Lady of Caversham Chapel, built on to Caversham's Our Lady and St Anne Church (South View Avenue) in 1959. St Anne's Well can be found at the top of Caversham's Priest Hill. St Peter's Church, which stands on high ground above gardens and allotments, includes a Norman doorway. The nearby rectory has a riverside garden from where a recent rector dived daily into the Thames every summer for 20 years.

After the bridge there is Reading Rowing Club (refreshment kiosk at the back). A clear, wide towpath runs along the bank with views of Caversham's church and substantial houses with boathouses.

Later, the way narrows at fields to pass St Mary's Island and later cross a boatyard. The railway comes close to the towpath as it passes Appletree Eyot and Poplar Island. Below Tilehurst Station the reach is known as the Kentwood Deeps. Leave the river at the Roebuck Hotel pub sign to climb steps over the railway while the towpath continues for a short distance to Roebuck Ferry Cottage before switching briefly to the left bank for the bend north.

> **The Roebuck** dates from the 17th century, when this was a coach stop on the Oxford–London road. It was being in enlarged in 1884 when the winning Cambridge boat race crew was based here during training. The restored building is now residential apartments.

Turn right along the main road to enter Purley-on-Thames. Follow the wall by the woodland and turn right through the gate to follow a woodland path down to Skerritt Way. Continue along the road. Ahead on the hill can be seen Purley Park mansion. At the end go left into Hazel Road. At a crossroads go right over the railway and down New Hill.

> **Purley** has long presented problems for anyone following the Thames. In the 1780s the Thames Commissioners faced opposition to a towpath from the owner of a riverside meadow and orchard in front of the church. In 1784 two ferries were established to enable the towpath to run on the opposite bank for 1/3 mile. The failure of the commissioners to carry through a threat of compulsory purchase caused the Countryside Commission much work 200 years later when preparing the Thames Path route. The church (at the eastern end of St Mary's Avenue) has a Norman chancel arch and font. Purley Park mansion, built in 1609, was home of Warren Hastings from 1788 to 1794, just before being rebuilt to a design by James Wyatt.

At the bottom of New Hill turn left and right to go up Mapledurham Drive, the access road for Mapledurham Lock. There is a gate halfway along, but just before the cattle-grid go ahead through a kissing gate and keep forward to the river. In winter Mapledurham House (on the far bank) can be seen through the trees. At the towpath go right for a short distance only for a good view of Mapledurham church and House. The Thames Path continues left through a gate to a footbridge leading to Mapledurham Lock.

On the left bank is the river's last working **mill**. The mansion was built in 1588 and remains occupied by the same family. (Neither can be reached on foot from the towpath.) The lock setting inspired some of EH Shepard's drawings for *The Wind in the Willows*, with Mapledurham House said, among others, to be the model for 'Toad Hall'.

The path runs alongside meadows passing through several gates. In the field after new Environment Agency gate 189 there is a brief view across the water to Hardwick House on the Oxfordshire bank.

Elizabeth I visited the **Hardwick House** soon after completion. Charles I played bowls on the lawn running down to the Thames towards the end of his troubled reign, when the house suffered damage in the Civil War. The Tudor house, in the hands of the Lybbe family until the end of the 19th century, is now the residence of Sir Julian Rose, who runs the estate farm on organic lines. His great-grandfather, Sir Charles, was the model for 'Toad' in *Wind in the Willows*, and the house is author Kenneth Grahame's most likely inspiration for 'Toad Hall'.

Later the towpath passes through the National Trust's Pangbourne Meadow before reaching lattice girder Whitchurch Bridge. To reach the town bear left at the bridge through a car park and go left along the road.

Hardwick House

FACILITIES INFORMATION – READING TO PANGBOURNE

Refreshments
Mapledurham Lock: Café. 11am–6pm on fine weekends Easter–Oct and
weekdays July–Aug.

Accommodation
Caversham Bridge: Premier Inn, Richfield Avenue RG1 8EQ
(0871 527 8922, www.premierinn.com).

Transport
Reading: National Rail.
Purley: National Rail from Tilehurst.
Pangbourne: National Rail.

Map
OS Explorer 159 (Reading) or 171 (Chiltern Hills West).

STAGE 12
Pangbourne to Goring

Start	Whitchurch Bridge
Finish	Goring Bridge
Distance	4 miles (6.4km)

At Whitchurch there is the Thames Path's longest diversion from the riverside and the only steep climb. This is because the towpath stays on the right bank until Gatehampton where the ferry has ceased to operate. The high walk is in woodland with views down on to the towpath before the river turns north to Goring Gap.

PANGBOURNE

Pangbourne is named after the River Pang which joins the Thames here. The village sign incorporates a copy of *The Wind in the Willows* by Kenneth Grahame who lived at Church Cottage, with the old village lock-up in the garden, from 1924 until his death in 1932. His funeral was at the next-door church, decorated with willows gathered that morning from the river. The St James the Less dedication may have originally been 'the Great' since the church belonged to Reading Abbey whose abbot had a house here. The tower was built in 1718 and the main church rebuilt in the 1860s. The Angel Gabriel in the west window featured on a 1992 Christmas stamp. DH Evans, founder of the department store, lived at Shooters Hill House (now the Masonic Hall) and built in 1896 the so-called 'seven deadly sins' – the houses facing the river upstream of the Swan. Malicious local gossip maintained that they were for Evans' mistresses. One occupant was society hostess Lady Cunard.

For 1:25K route map see booklet pages 42–44.

Cross the bridge from Berkshire to Oxfordshire to enter Whitchurch-on-Thames.

Although there was a ferry at **Whitchurch** the river could be forded until the 1790s when the channel was dredged to accommodate barges from the new Thames and Severn Canal. The first bridge, steep and wooden, was built in 1792. The present iron bridge opened in 1902 and is one of only two Thames bridges maintaining tolls (see Stage 17). Pedestrians, sheep, boars and pigs used to be charged ½d each. Carriages were 2d 'for each and every wheel' and today cars are charged 20p but since decimalisation walkers cross free. The church dates from Norman times but is largely Victorian – a north aisle window shows Jesus at work with a saw in his stepfather's workshop.

Before the Whitchurch-on-Thames sign go left to enter the driveway to the Mill. To the left there is a view across the water to the bridge. Beyond the cottage turn right up a sheltered walled footpath running to the churchyard. Beyond the lychgate keep forward past Walliscote Lodge to return to the road.

Turn left to pass the Greyhound. The street climbs the hill and just beyond the art gallery (left) the pavement ends. Keep on past the White House (left) to turn left along a hard surface public bridleway. Follow the metalled lane for ½ mile to where the way bends left to Hartslock Farm. Here continue ahead down a steep stepped path into a valley. The enclosed path climbs up between fields. On entering Hartslock Wood follow a

Pangbourne village lock-up

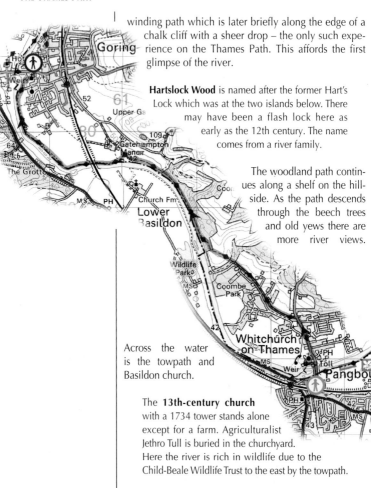

winding path which is later briefly along the edge of a chalk cliff with a sheer drop – the only such experience on the Thames Path. This affords the first glimpse of the river.

Hartslock Wood is named after the former Hart's Lock which was at the two islands below. There may have been a flash lock here as early as the 12th century. The name comes from a river family.

The woodland path continues along a shelf on the hillside. As the path descends through the beech trees and old yews there are more river views.

Across the water is the towpath and Basildon church.

The **13th-century church** with a 1734 tower stands alone except for a farm. Agriculturalist Jethro Tull is buried in the churchyard. Here the river is rich in wildlife due to the Child-Beale Wildlife Trust to the east by the towpath.

Where the ground levels out the path becomes enclosed as it runs along the side of a field. Here the path is a little way from the river, but just before reaching Gatehampton Farm turn left. Beyond a backwater bridge is Ferry Cottage (left).

At **Gatehampton** the towpath comes over from the Basildon bank. This spot has been under almost continuous occupation. Stone Age relics have been discovered, and the earliest evidence of post-glacial man in Britain has been found near the railway which cuts through the site of a Roman grain drier.

Turn right to follow the returned towpath and go under the railway bridge. A gate leads into Little Meadow and at the far end go through another gate. The Goring Gap hills can be seen half right. As the ground indicates, many walkers cut the corner, although the towpath stays with the riverbank. After the towpath leaves the fields it passes three well-spaced and charming boathouses. Soon there is a view of Streatley Bridge before the path passes an old ferry point (grass picnic area) and the moorings. Cross the mill stream and go right up the side of Goring Bridge.

FACILITIES INFORMATION – PANGBOURNE TO GORING

Refreshments

Pangbourne: Laughing Halibut Fish and Chip Shop, 16 Whitchurch Road. Mon–Sat 11.30am–2pm; daily 4.30–10pm.

Whitchurch: The Ferryboat, High Street. Tue–Sat 12pm–3pm and 6pm–11pm; Sun 12pm–3pm. Food Tue–Sat 12–2.30pm.

Accommodation

Pangbourne: Weir View House, Shooters Hill, RG8 7BJ (0118 9842120, www.weirview.co.uk).

Transport

Pangbourne: National Rail.

Goring: National Rail from Goring and Streatley Station.

Maps

OS Explorer 171 (Chiltern Hills West).

STAGE 13
Goring to Wallingford

Start	Goring Bridge
Finish	Wallingford Bridge
Distance	7 miles (11.2km)

This stretch has both the shortest and the longest reach between locks. At Goring the river comes out of the long gorge into a plateau rich in wildfowl. Runsford Hole is the first of two holes in this chapter – hole means 'a place where water is deep'.

GORING

The Norman church, later dedicated to St Thomas Becket, was part of a convent – corbels on the south outside wall supported a cloister roof. Inside a bell dates from about 1290, and the rood screen from just 1912 is made from wood from HMS *Thunderer* of Nelson's fleet. Oscar Wilde spent the summer of 1893 at Ferry Cottage, and his play *An Ideal Husband* includes references to the area, such as 'Viscount Goring' and 'Countess Basildon'. The cottage was later enlarged to become the home of Sir Arthur 'Bomber' Harris who died here in 1984. The mill, mentioned in the Domesday Book, is the subject of an unfinished painting by Turner. The village is unusual in retaining several shops.

For 1:25K route map see booklet pages 39–40.

Oxford's Magdalen College barge at Streatley

Cross the bridge to leave Oxfordshire and reach Streatley on the Berkshire bank.

Since the ancient Ridgeway (or Icknield Way from the Wash to Wiltshire) crosses here there must have been a ford here from early times. A ferry was running from at least Henry I's time, but the river continued to be forded until 1797, when the building of Goring Lock raised the water level. This made the ferry crossing more dangerous and there were deaths when the ferry boat overturned in 1810. The first bridge opened in 1838 with a tollgate on the central island. The **present bridge** dates from 1923.

Streatley means 'road', referring to the Ridgeway. In the 1830s Moses Saunders, the last ferryman, was innkeeper at the Swan. His boat-building business eventually moved to Cowes to become the famous Saunders-Rowe. The Swan, although on the Berkshire bank, is partly in Oxfordshire because the mill, which stood across the road, belonged to Goring's convent. The church was rebuilt in the 13th century by Bishop Poore of Salisbury, who was responsible for his new cathedral and its spire, but here the tower was added 200 years later. Streatley House in the main street dates from about 1765 and was home of the Morrell family – relatives of the Bloomsbury Group's Lady Ottoline.

Map continues on page 140

139

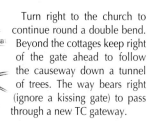

Turn right to the church to continue round a double bend. Beyond the cottages keep right of the gate ahead to follow the causeway down a tunnel of trees. The way bears right (ignore a kissing gate) to pass through a new TC gateway.

Streatley TC Gate was replaced by the National Rivers Authority (NRA). It is rare to see a Conservancy/NRA/ Environment Agency towpath gate away from the river, but this inland path is the towpath. Towing horses were led over the bridge and along this route while their barges were poled across the river.

Cross a low footbridge and bear round to the left with the stones to find a gate by the river. Beyond another gate the towpath crosses a drawbridge at an inlet. Soon the path is alongside the track to Cleeve Lock.

On the far bank is the 17th-century four-bedroom **Cleeve Mill** which generates its own electricity.

Soon there is a view from a meadow across to the whitewashed Leatherne Bottel below a cliff.

The Leatherne Bottel was popular in the 16th and 17th centuries for its water from a spring which had been known to the Romans. The pub is now a noted restaurant where diners have included celebrities such as Emma Thompson, Kenneth Branagh, George Cole, Willie Carson and Keith Floyd. Its garden supplies herbs and vegetables.

At the far end of the meadow go through the gate and pass a willow copse at Runsford Hole to pass out of

Boathouse at Goring

Heron at Runsford Hole

Berkshire into Oxfordshire (but still Berkshire until 1974). Soon after there is a view of South Stoke church beyond the far bank. The way is alongside a wood before passing the Egyptian House and reaching the Beetle and Wedge at Moulsford.

MOULSFORD

At the end of the 19th century water was so low one summer that carts laden with the harvest forded here as they must have done when Moulsford was a 'mules ford'. The Beetle and Wedge pub, a riverside hotel on a former timber wharf, is named after the 'beetle', or mallet, used for driving a wedge into logs for splitting before being floated downstream. This is 'the Potwell Inn' in HG Wells' *History of Mr Polly*, which he wrote here. It also features in Jerome's *Three Men in a Boat*. Bernard Shaw often stayed when the landlord ran the ferry for the towpath, which switches banks here. In the early 19th century it cost 1½d to take a towing horse across. The Manor House is featured in ITV's *Midsomer Murders*. The next-door small 1847 church by George Gilbert Scott is on the site of a 12th-century church. The Egyptian House, completed in 2000, is a concrete building designed by John Outram to replace a 1970s building.

Turn inland between the pub buildings to walk up Ferry Lane to a crossroads. Turn right along the main road. Just beyond Moulsford Preparatory School's playing field, go right through a gate into Offlands Farm. Follow the hedged track downhill. At the bottom the way turns left to become a wide way above a field. Ahead is the Paddington–Oxford railway line on a high bank. Bear right towards a farm gate, but go through the kissing gate in the green fence. Follow a narrow path to go over a wooden footbridge beneath the railway bridge to join the riverbank. A wooded path runs ahead near, but not close to, the bank. A one point the way is down steps. At Littlestoke Ferry go through the kissing gates to rejoin the towpath which returns from the far bank. (Go left up Ferry Lane only for the Morning Star pub and Cholsey Station beyond the main road.) The main path, while in the nature reserve, tends to run a little away from the bank. There are several redundant gateways before the path passes through a kissing gate, creating a brief double bend, and is level with North Stoke on the left bank.

North Stoke, ½ mile upstream from the old ferry, is almost hidden. The church tower was built in 1725, but at the base are medieval wall paintings. Its dedication is St Mary of Bec, following the wedding there of a local Saxon lord to a Norman baron's daughter. The 17th-century Rectory Farmhouse was recently the home of actor Michael Caine who was born downstream at Rotherhithe.

Soon after a gateway at a footbridge by a wood, the path is over several gardens. The way draws level with Mongewell Park, opposite, shortly before the road bridge.

Mongewell Park came into the hands of Shute Barrington in 1770, a year after he became Bishop of Llandaff. He was translated to Salisbury before becoming, for 35 years until his death in 1826, Bishop of Durham. He had married the daughter of the previous owner, Sir John Guise. The Georgian mansion was demolished in 1890, but the chapel, where the bishop is buried, survives by the river – upstream of the inlet. In winter the estate's ice house would be filled with at least 20 cart loads of ice from the Thames. The modern buildings were part of Carmel College, the Jewish school, founded in 1948 and closed in 1997.

Soon after the path passes under the 1993 Wallingford bypass bridge. At Chalmore Hole the towpath is suddenly enclosed.

The Thames Conservancy building on the left is a reminder of **Wallingford Lock**, which existed from 1838 to 1883 but was only used at times of very low water. Jerome in *Three Men in a Boat* is confused when he fails to find the lock.

The way ahead is now a footpath, while the towpath continues on the left bank – a ferry was introduced after the lock's removal. Continue over Oxford University Boat

Mongewell Park boathouse

Club's swing bridge and ahead through a break in the hedge. At Lower Wharf go round a bend and at once turn right to go under an archway in a house and over the millstream. A path runs behind Wallingford's St Leonard's Church. Turn right along Thames Street to reach the main road. The town centre is to the left but the Thames Path continues to the right to Wallingford Bridge.

FACILITIES INFORMATION – GORING TO WALLINGFORD

Refreshments
Goring: The Miller of Mansfield, High Street, RG8 9AW.
Goring: Pierreponts Café, River Bridge Approach. Tue–Sat 8am–5pm.

Accommodation
Goring: Miller of Mansfield, High Street, RG8 9AW (01491 872829,
   www.millerofmansfield.com).
Goring: Melrose Cottage, 36 Milldown Road, RG8 0BD (01491 873040).
Streatley: YHA, Reading Road, RG8 9JJ (0845 371 9044, www.yha.org.uk).
Streatley: Stable Cottage, RG8 9JX (01491 874408).

Transport
Goring: National Rail to Goring and Streatley Station.
Moulsford: National Rail from Cholsey (turn left at Ferry Lane at north end of
   village).
Wallingford: Bus (www.traveline.info; 0871 200 2233) to Cholsey Station.
   On certain days there are steam trains from Wallingford to Cholsey Station
   (information 01491 835067, www.cholsey-wallingford-railway.com).

Tourist Information
Wallingford: Town Hall, Market Place, OX10 0EG (01491 826972).

Maps
OS Explorer 170 (Abingdon) or 171 (Chiltern Hills West).

STAGE 14
Wallingford to Dorchester

Start	Wallingford Bridge
Finish	River Thame/Thames confluence
	(SU 577 932)
Distance	5 miles (8km)

This is a short walk by way of Benson and Shillingford to reach the confluence of the Thames and Thame beneath the Sinodun Hills. Nearby is Dorchester, dominated by its huge church, where the monastic guesthouse maintains the tradition of hospitality by serving teas.

WALLINGFORD

Wallingford, meaning 'Welsh people's ford', is on the London–Wales road. A chamberlain appointed annually is in charge of the bridge dating from the 13th century. There was both a wooden bridge and a ford when William the Conqueror crossed here in 1066 on his journey from Hastings to London. Next year he ordered the building of the castle where later Chaucer's son was constable. The castle, open in summer, was reduced to its ruined state in 1646 by Cromwell after a 16-week siege. The George and Dragon, dating from 1517, has tears drawn on a wall by a landlord's daughter who saw her Royalist soldier fiancé stabbed in the bar. The town once had eleven parish churches. The redundant St Peter's with its candle snuffer steeple was designed by Sir Robert Taylor in 1777, although some suggest that jurist Sir William Blackstone who lived at riverside Castle Priory suggested the tower. The Market Place is dominated by the 1670 Town Hall in front of St Mary-le-More from where a curfew is rung. The weekly Friday market dates from an 1155 Henry I charter – the 1153 Treaty of Wallingford had confirmed the Plantagenet succession. William Morris stayed at the Town Arms in 1880 on his trip between his riverside houses at Hammersmith and Kelmscott. Artist George Dunlop Leslie lived at Riverside in Thames Street from 1884 to 1907. Actress Sheila Hancock was taught to swim in the Thames when a young wartime evacuee.

Spire of St Peter's Church at Wallingford

At Wallingford Bridge turn down Castle Lane at the side of the Town Arms and bear right at the back. The towpath runs alongside the castle's meadows, known as the Queen's Arbour and King's Meadow. After a gate the path is set back from the once badly eroded bank.

The now firm way runs directly to a sharp right turn at a wooden footbridge leading to Benson Lock. Cross the

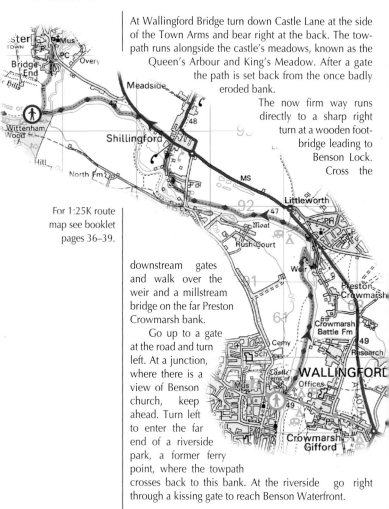

For 1:25K route map see booklet pages 36–39.

downstream gates and walk over the weir and a millstream bridge on the far Preston Crowmarsh bank.

Go up to a gate at the road and turn left. At a junction, where there is a view of Benson church, keep ahead. Turn left to enter the far end of a riverside park, a former ferry point, where the towpath crosses back to this bank. At the riverside go right through a kissing gate to reach Benson Waterfront.

The partly Norman church was under Dorchester Abbey until 1534. The clock, added in 1794, is said to have come from Horse Guards in Whitehall.

During the Civil War Charles I held a privy council meeting at the Red Lion, now Monarch Court House private residence. **Benson**, once called Bensington, was on the edge of marshland – the footpath alongside Ferry Road is called the High Path since the river used to flood the road. On the riverside are recorded the distances to London Bridge (92 miles) and Cricklade (63 miles).

Continue through the boatyard to a caravan park. Keep on the lower path to reach a kissing gate. From here the towpath is alongside meadows with a view of the riverside garden wall of Rush Court on the far bank. Later the towpath is by a fence as it approaches Shillingford Bridge with a view of the hotel.

Shillingford Bridge, one of the finest on the river, is exactly halfway between Reading and Oxford and Windsor and Lechlade. There was probably a short-lived wooden bridge here in the 14th century. Another wooden structure was thrown across in the 1780s. The present balustraded stone crossing was built in 1827. The Shillingford Bridge Hotel was once the Swan Inn, welcoming 'rowing and picnic parties'. The 'Shilling-ford' was probably Roman and upstream beyond Shillingford Wharf.

At the bridge go inland to climb up to the road. Leave the towpath (which crosses the bridge) and go ahead along the road for a very short distance. At Ferry House go left down a road, marked 'private', to pass an entrance to Bridge House. At the divide go right, and just before the High Trees gateway go right again through the kissing gate. Follow the narrow enclosed path, and beyond Shillingford Court turn left along a short passage to reach Shillingford Wharf.

Shillingford Wharf was once used by a brewery (opposite the Kingfisher at the far end of the road) and coal was landed here for Warborough to the

north. In the 1980s *Church Times* editor John Whale
undertook an annual August swim from here to
Shillingford Bridge. The towpath is on the far bank
and crosses back upstream at the former Keen Edge
Ferry. 'Keen' comes from 'cane', meaning 'willows'.
WB Yeats stayed at Wheeler's End (timber-framed on
west side of road north of crossroads) in summer
1921 while beginning the poem *Meditations in Time
of Civil War*.

Walk the length of Wharf Road to the crossroads by
the Kingfisher. Turn left along the main road – at the bus
stop it is necessary to cross over to follow the pavement
from where there is soon an early view of Dorchester
Abbey. Once past the two houses look out for a gateway
on the left, just opposite the huge traffic sign.

Cross the road with care to go through the kissing gate and ahead to rejoin the towpath, which
crossed back at Keen Edge Ferry. Turn right to continue
upstream. Later the towpath crosses the River Thame
entrance at a gated bridge.

The River Thame rises just north of Aylesbury in
Buckinghamshire. The river's sheltered entrance is
a popular mooring, although it is difficult to sail as
far as Dorchester. It was in the Thame near here that
St Birinus baptised King Cynegils of Wessex. Some
have insisted that 'Thames' comes from an amalga-
mation of 'Thame' and 'Isis'. The latter is the Oxford
name for the Thames. Others simply say that from
this confluence to just beyond Oxford the river is
the 'Isis' rather than 'Thames'. This may derive from
'Thamesis', the Latin for Thames.

Beyond the bridge a path runs inland towards a stile
and on to nearby Dorchester, while the Thames Path continues on the towpath with Little Wittenham Wood on
the far bank.

FACILITIES INFORMATION – WALLINGFORD TO DORCHESTER

Refreshments
Wallingford: Greggs, Market Place. Open weekdays.
Benson: Waterfront café. Open daily (also laundrette).

Accommodation
Wallingford: Little Gables, 166 Crowmarsh Hill, OX10 8BG (01491 837834,
  www.littlegables.co.uk).
Wallingford: 52 Blackstone Road OX10 8JL (01491 839339).
Wallingford: Bridge Villa campsite on Crowmarsh bank: Feb–Dec
  (01491 836860).
Benson: Waterfront Camping Park, OX10 6SJ (01491 838304). Apr–Oct.
Shillingford Bridge: Bridge House 0X10 7EU (01865 858540,
  www.bridge-house.org.uk). Christian community following green guidelines.
Shillingford: Marsh House, Court Drive, OX10 7ER (01865 858496).
  Turn right by Shillingford Court before Wharf.
Shillingford: The Kingfisher Inn OX10 7EL (01865 858595,
  www.kingfisher-inn.co.uk).

Transport
Wallingford: Bus (www.traveline.info; 0871 200 2233) from Cholsey Station.
  On certain days there are steam trains from Wallingford to Cholsey Station
  (information 01491 835067,
  www.cholsey-wallingford-railway.com).
Dorchester: Bus (www.traveline.info; 0871 200 2233) to Oxford or Cholsey
  then National Rail.

Tourist Information
Wallingford: Town Hall, Market Place, OX10 0EG (01491 826972).

Maps
OS Explorer 170 (Abingdon).

STAGE 15

Dorchester to Abingdon

Start	River Thame/Thames confluence (SU 577 932)
Finish	Abingdon Bridge
Distance	9 miles (14.5km)

Dorchester lies on high ground across fields from the Thames. The three miles between Day's Lock and Clifton Hampden is along flood meadows and therefore liable to be occasionally under water in winter. The full nine miles is a lonely stretch with only one riverside village, although there are pubs in nearby hidden villages.

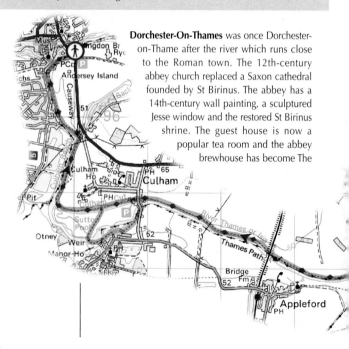

Dorchester-On-Thames was once Dorchester-on-Thame after the river which runs close to the Roman town. The 12th-century abbey church replaced a Saxon cathedral founded by St Birinus. The abbey has a 14th-century wall painting, a sculptured Jesse window and the restored St Birinus shrine. The guest house is now a popular tea room and the abbey brewhouse has become The

George Hotel – one of ten inns in the 18th century serving the Oxford–London coaches. On the path to the Thames is St Birinus' Church, built in 1849 to a design by Pugin follower William Wilkinson Wardell whose other work includes Melbourne Cathedral.

For 1:25K route map see booklet pages 32–36.

(**Route out of Dorchester to River** Leave the abbey church by the south gate, next to the the tollhouse, and bear left. Just before the bridge go left to find a hidden path which runs down to a tunnel. Once through the low passage turn left to pass St Birinus' Church.

Continue ahead to keep on the right side of the green. Keep forward, but before reaching a thatched cottage ahead go sharp right under a barrier and up a short path. At the end go left, and where the way divides keep forward (but not directly ahead) on a footpath running down the side of a field. Go over a wooden stile at the end to continue south. Stay near the field boundary to the left to bear round the corner of the oddly shaped field and

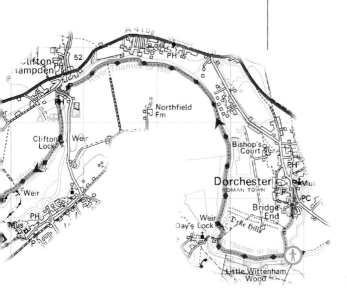

find a stile ahead. Still continue forward to meet the River Thame at a bend and follow the bank to its confluence with the Thames.)

Where the rivers Thame and Thames meet, take the Thames Path upstream with Little Wittenham Wood to the left on the far bank. Soon the Thames turns north to Day's Lock beneath Little Wittenham.

> The church at **Little Wittenham**, which has a 15th-century tower, was once a daughter church of Abingdon Abbey. Opposite, a path leads up to Wittenham Clumps on the Sinodun Hills – the local name is 'Mother Daunch's Buttocks', after Oliver Cromwell's aunt who lived at the Manor House next to the church. The beech trees are partly in an Iron Age fort. Artist Paul Nash first drew the Clumps in 1912, and his later oil version, *Landscape of the Vernal Equinox*, is in the Royal Collection, having been purchased by the Queen Mother. The bridge to the hamlet is the scene of the annual International Pooh Sticks Championships, held here since 1984 – apart from 1997 when the river was frozen. Upstream Day's Lock acquired its name in the 1820s from a lock keeper.

After passing under the bridge keep ahead to find a kissing gate at the far end of the lock compound. Here the Thames Path crosses the upstream lock gates and the weir to the right bank. (Meanwhile the historic towpath continues on the left bank for a few more yards to a former ferry point at the end of the earthwork.)

The Thames Path joins the line of the towpath as the river begins a long arch westwards round the edge of meadows grazed by cattle with access to the river. On the way the path later has a view across to Burcot back gardens on the far bank.

> **Burcot** is easily missed on the far side of the Thames behind long gardens, but until 1636 this was, due to shallow water and a hard sandstone river bed,

Clifton Hampden churchyard and Manor House

the end of navigation, where passengers and goods took to the road for Oxford and beyond. There is evidence of Roman occupation here.

On approaching Clifton Hampden there is, level with the stile, a lonely cross on the far bank, and soon after a view of Clifton Manor House up on a high cliff near the church. The path curves inland to the road and runs up to a gate. Go right, across the bridge leading into the village (but turn left for the Barley Mow round the corner).

Clifton Hampden was once owned by the Hampden family, but the village owes its thatched look and bridge to Lord Aldenham, Governor of the Bank of England, who inherited the village in 1842. The water was so shallow here that cattle were driven across the ferry point, and in 1826 the Lord Mayor's barge became stuck on returning from Oxford. When the building of the upstream lock in 1835 raised the level, the ferry (run by Oxford's Exeter College since 1493) was replaced in 1864 by the bridge, built of local brick

155

Clifton Hampden Bridge

and designed by George Gilbert Scott, who had sketched a plan on his starched shirt cuff. He also remodelled the church, dating from at least 1180, and added the cliff-top vicarage which is now the the Manor House. The Barley Mow features in Jerome's *Three Men in a Boat* as 'the quaintest, most old-world inn up the river'. Bridge tolls were collected in person by the two nieces of Lord Aldenham until 1946.

At the north end of the bridge go down the slope to follow the towpath up to nearby Clifton Lock at the start of Clifton Cut.

Clifton Cut, opened in 1822 following the success of the upstream Culham Cut, bypasses straggling Long Wittenham which is reached only by way of Clifton Hampden Bridge.

The towpath continues along Clifton Cut while the Old Thames meanders south. Beyond the weir at the end of the cut, the path is alongside fields with a view of the church tower at Appleford across the river. After a copse the path passes under Appleford railway bridge on the

Paddington–Oxford line. There are views south to Didcot Power Station and Wittenham Clumps. On approaching Culham the way rises to run through trees. Stay by the water when the path divides to have a view of Sutton Courtenay Bridge where the river turns south to Sutton Courtenay, while ahead is the start of Culham Cut.

> **Culham Cut** was opened in 1809 to avoid the tortuous route through Sutton Courtenay to the south. Sutton Courtenay Bridge replaced a ferry in 1811.

Sutton Courtenay Diversion
To follow the old route through Sutton Courtenay, turn left over Sutton Courtenay Bridge and at the cottages cross the road to go through a kissing gate on the right. The path follows the Old Thames until the water becomes hidden by a hedge. At a stile go ahead down a drive and over a stile opposite the Fish in the village.

> **Sutton** was given to the de Courtenay family in the Norman period. Norman Hall is near the church. The present Manor House was the home until 2001 of David Astor, former editor and director of the *Observer*. The abbey, now a retreat house, was a grange belonging to Abingdon Abbey. Lord Asquith, the last Liberal prime minister, lived at the Wharf and is buried in the churchyard along with author George Orwell (Eric Blair; near the far-right corner). The Wharf recalls the time when barges called here, passing through a lock by a now disappeared mill, before the cut was made. The Fish was built in 1890 to replace a 17th-century inn destroyed by fire.

The exit from the village is along to the right just beyond the wall postbox at the corner. The path crosses a series of weir bridges. Beyond the main and last crossing bear half right across fields to a bridge spanning the lock cut. Ahead is Culham with Abingdon's St Helen's Church in the distance. Cross the bridge to rejoin the towpath and turn left.

The Thames Path continues over the road at Culham Bridge and past Culham Lock at the start of Culham Cut. Just before the next bridge (where walkers from Sutton Courtenay rejoin the main route) there is a turning to Culham village.

> The Manor House at **Culham**, which once belonged to Abingdon Abbey, has a 1685 dovecot with 4000 nesting places. The church is now largely Victorian, although the tower was rebuilt earlier in 1710. The Sow and Pigs on the green has become the Lion Inn. Culham College, founded in 1852, closed in 1979, but the Victorian Gothic building survives as a school. Until around 1400 the village spread over the field to the west with streets and passageways leading down to the river on two sides.

Where the present village ends the towpath crosses the abutment of an old bridge. As the cut ends the river turns sharply north. At the end of the open field cross a footbridge spanning the entrance to the Swift Ditch.

> **Swift Ditch** was cut by Abingdon Abbey in 1052. 'Swift' means 'short cut'. The 1½ mile cut was the main navigation channel until 1550 and again from 1635 to 1790. Barges moored overnight in specially dug pools. The island created by the cut is known as Aldersey Island, which is derived from its lost church of St Andrew. The 1416 bridge, carrying the main road until 1928, is just upstream from the southern end.

The towpath is alongside the meadows opposite Abingdon with a view of Abingdon School boathouse, erected in 2003 and Europe's largest oak building. Later there is the confluence with the River Ock and then St Helen's with its almshouses to be seen before Abingdon Bridge is reached.

St Helen's at Abingdon

FACILITIES INFORMATION – DORCHESTER TO ABINGDON

Refreshments
Dorchester: Abbey Tea Rooms. Wed, Thu, Sat and Sun Apr–Sept 3–5pm
or earlier if cake runs out.
Clifton Hampden: The Barley Mow, right bank. Chef and Brewer
11.30am–11pm (Sun 12–10pm) Food 12–10pm.
Sutton Courtenay: The George & Dragon (next to church). Mon–Fri
2pm–2.30pm and 6.30pm–9pm; weekends all day.

Accommodation
Clifton Hampden: camping at Bridge House Caravan Site, Bridge House,
OX14 3EH (01865 407725).
Sutton Courtenany: Bekynton House, 7 The Green, OX14 4AF (01235 848888).

Transport
Dorchester: National Rail to Oxford or Cholsey then bus (www.traveline.info;
0871 200 2233).
Abingdon: Bus (www.traveline.info; 0871 200 2233) to Oxford then
National Rail.

Tourist Information
Abingdon: Old Abbey House, OX14 3JD (01235 522711).

Map
OS Explorer 170 (Abingdon).

STAGE 16

Abingdon to Oxford

Start	Abingdon Bridge
Finish	Osney Bridge, Oxford
Distance	9½ miles (15.2km)

This is a lonely stretch and until recently it was inaccessible from Abingdon. Lewis Carroll often walked the towpath from Oxford as far as Radley where his friend was vicar. Around Radley the college oarsmen flash past rushes, harvested every July for chair seating by Tony Handley of Country Chairmen, who is the only supplier of native freshwater rushes. Salisbury Cathedral's chairs have Thames rush seats. The same patch is cut only every three years, so sometimes the team of around fourteen harvesters camp as far upstream as Tadpole or Rushey above Oxford. The towpath becomes firmer and busier on approaching Oxford where there is, of course, more rowing.

ABINGDON

Abingdon is one of the oldest continuously inhabited towns in Britain. The Benedictine abbey was here from 695 until 1538. The abbey church has disappeared, but some monastic buildings remain at the end of Thames Street, which runs parallel with the Abbey Stream, dug in the 10th century. Upper Reaches Hotel was the mill house. The gateway is beside St Nicholas' Church which was the abbey's church for the laity. Outside is a plaque in honour of Abingdon-born St Edmund of Abingdon who became Archbishop of Canterbury in 1233. St Helen's by the river has a 14th-century Lady Chapel ceiling with fine examples of medieval iconography – surviving both the Reformation and Cromwell because it was too high to reach. One of the three adjoining almshouse blocks dates from 1446. Monday has been market day since 1086. County Hall, built between 1678 and 1682 by Christopher Kempster, Wren's master mason at St Paul's, recalls that this was Berkshire's county town until 1867. Morland Brewery was founded here in 1711. MG cars (Morris Garages) were manufactured here from 1929 until 1980. The Michaelmas Fair (Mon–Tues before 11 Oct) is Europe's longest street fair – the smaller Runaway Fair a week later has its origins in the chance for labour hired at the main fair to seek another employer.

Abingdon County Hall

Start at the meadows end of Abingdon Bridge opposite the town. Follow the towpath (which runs under the bridge) to reach a gate at Abingdon Lock. Leave the towpath by crossing over the lower lock gates, the lock island and the weir to reach the Abingdon bank.

For 1:25K route map see booklet pages 29–32.

Map continues on page 165

Follow the Abbey Stream (right) to go over a wooden bridge. At a path junction go right. The path follows a ditch (right). Soon after crossing to the opposite side, the path curves round a long inlet. Bear right (ignoring a permissive path to the left) and at another fork go left. Soon the trees to the right fall away to reveal the river shortly before the point where the towpath switches from the far side. There is a view of the Swift Ditch weir and entrance and, in the distance between trees, St Helen's spire in Abingdon. The path has occasional picnic tables and is at first wooded. After Nuneham Railway Bridge, the far bank is heavily wooded. The way is level with Lock Wood Island when it passes through TC gate 102.

Lock Wood Island may not be natural, as there was a lock here from at least Elizabethan times until early in the 19th century. The lock channel was by the left bank, although the

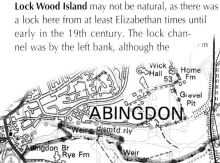

Abingdon Bridge

main channel is now on the right by the towpath. This was a popular spot, with the thatched lock cottage becoming a tearoom and reached by a rustic bridge. The lonely Old Boathouse residence above the island is the original late-19th-century Radley College Dry Boathouse.

A high bridge carries the path over a boathouse entrance. Shortly after the Old Boathouse there is a framed view of Nuneham House, and to the right can be seen the Carfax Conduit up on a wooded hill.

Nuneham was 'New Ham'. The riverside was landscaped in the 1770s by Capability Brown, when the core of the house was built for the first Lord Harcourt. The nearby temple-style building is a church designed by Harcourt. The Carfax Conduit stood in Oxford as part of the water supply system from 1615 to 1786. Author Lewis Carroll organised river trips from Oxford to here for picnics in the woods when the party included the original Alice. More recently the house was used by Oxford University.

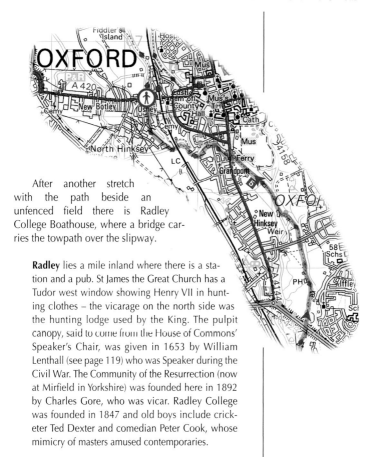

After another stretch with the path beside an unfenced field there is Radley College Boathouse, where a bridge carries the towpath over the slipway.

Radley lies a mile inland where there is a station and a pub. St James the Great Church has a Tudor west window showing Henry VII in hunting clothes – the vicarage on the north side was the hunting lodge used by the King. The pulpit canopy, said to come from the House of Commons' Speaker's Chair, was given in 1653 by William Lenthall (see page 119) who was Speaker during the Civil War. The Community of the Resurrection (now at Mirfield in Yorkshire) was founded here in 1892 by Charles Gore, who was vicar. Radley College was founded in 1847 and old boys include cricketer Ted Dexter and comedian Peter Cook, whose mimicry of masters amused contemporaries.

There are more fields and after 1½ miles the path reaches a car park at Sandford. Cross the footbridge over the wide weir channel to reach the lock. On the far side is a housing block, replacing a mill, and the King's Arms.

In 1240 Thomas de Saunford gave the manor at **Sandford** to the Knights Templar, whose preceptory

Nuneham House boathouse

remains just north of the village on the left bank. In 1862 Lewis Carroll, having walked from Oxford to Radley and back to here, preached his first sermon at the partly Norman church. A mill operated here from 1294 until 1982, having in its last years produced coloured paper. The King's Arms site has been an inn since the 15th century. The lock is the deepest on the river and one of the oldest. Michael Llewelyn-Davies, JM Barrie's inspiration for Peter Pan, drowned in the fierce 'Sandford Lasher' weir upstream just 68 years after Jerome K Jerome had written in *Three Men in a Boat*: 'The pool under Sandford Lasher, just behind the lock, is a very good place to drown yourself in.'

The towpath continues beyond a TC gate, and just before the way becomes enclosed there is a view of Sandford church tower. The path crosses two weir bridges before continuing along the lock island. A little further on the towpath bears left to cross the main weir stream entrance. After a TC gateway there is a choice of paths, for while the towpath remains faithful to the river there is a public footpath cutting the corner as the river double bends at Rose Isle.

Rose Isle was known in the 19th century as both St Michael's Island and Kennington Island, after the village behind the railway on the right bank. The present house replaced the Swan Inn.

After the two paths have merged there is the last section of grass towpath until after Oxford. Go through a kissing gate at a railway bridge.

Kennington Railway Bridge carried the Oxford–High Wycombe branch line, opened in 1864. Now the track runs only as far as Cowley. The present bridge was built in 1923 immediately downstream of the old abutments. The new towpath bridge immediately upstream, crossing the weir's mill-stream, replaces a 1920s structure.

After the bridge, the towpath is alongside a wood before passing under Isis Bridge (1962). Ahead is Iffley Lock and alongside the path are the Iffley Meadows. Across the water there is a brief view of Iffley church.

The origin of the name **Iffley** is uncertain. The church is an outstanding Norman example, built about 1170. The stone decoration has links with sculpture once found at Reading Abbey, and a doorway has flowers found elsewhere only in the cathedral porch at Santiago de Compostela. Recent sensitive interior changes include in 1995 replacing Victorian glass with a John Piper design. Until the middle of the 20th century funeral processions came by river – bodies could not be carried over the lock for fear of creating a right of way. The mill was burnt down in 1908, but some mill stones remain outside Grist Cottage and Mill

College barge near Oxford

House Garden in Mill Lane by the weir. The lock, one of the oldest pound locks dating from 1632, was rebuilt in 1923 with rollers (by the towpath) for punts.

Just round the corner on the towpath there is the the Isis Tavern.

The Isis was built as a farmhouse in about 1800 and became an inn in 1842. The interior is decorated with plenty of oars and there is a skittle alley. Until 1979 beer was delivered by punt. Artist Peter de Wint (1784–1849) painted the view, a little upstream from the towpath, of the inn with Iffley church in the background. The house's surrounding farmland is wet meadowland noted for the rare snake's head (or fritillary), flowering in late spring. Also found here are marsh marigold, meadow buttercup and oxeye daisy.

At the end of the meadow the towpath runs under Donnington Bridge (1926). St John's College barge may be moored in a backwater on the far side. Soon after passing the Oxford City boundary stone, where the river is known by rowers as the Gut, the Isis (as the Thames is called here) suddenly widens as the right bank swings round to the two footbridges at Longbridges. The boathouse next door belongs to Hertford College. Ahead can be seen more boathouses and the first Oxford spire – Christ Church. The towpath is alongside more meadows. Shortly, on the far bank the River Cherwell joins the Thames on the two sides of the line of college boathouses. On the towpath is the remains of the Oxford University Boat Club.

The **River Cherwell** entered the Thames only at the higher confluence until the new cut was made downstream in 1884. This new and now main channel was necessary because the river flows were opposed to each other. When the Cherwell was fast-flowing in 1663 the Thames was driven back a mile, causing a tidal bore. On other occasions a fast-flowing Thames often drove back the Cherwell, causing flooding.

Oxford boathouses

Oxford University Boat Club building opened in 1881 and was destroyed by fire in 1999. The club produces the crew for the annual boat race in London, as well as organising rowing within the university, including the Bumping Races at the end of May. The boathouses opposite date from the 1930s and succeeded the college barges which were moored there.

There is a view across the water to Christ Church Meadow before the path crosses a footbridge with a view (left) of water flowing under Grandpont House.

Grandpont House, where a braid of the Thames flows underneath, was built in 1785 for Oxford's town clerk, Sir William Elias Taunton. Almost a century later it was the residence of Alderman Thomas Randall, a hatter and unpopular magistrate who attempted to restrict pub opening hours. It remains a residence.

*Christ Church
Meadow*

Beyond Isis House the towpath crosses another bridge and bears left to run up on to Oxford's Folly Bridge.

Folly Bridge, the southern entry to Oxford, was built in 1827. The name recalls a tower which stood on the previous structure and not the present Caudwell's Castle, built in 1849. Folly Bridge Store on the north end was built in 1844 as the tollhouse, but free passage has been allowed since 1850. Salter Brothers, established in 1858, still operate from here, although its former boatyard, originally an 1830 warehouse for goods sent by river to and from London, is now the Head of the River pub. Lewis Carroll set out from here in July 1862 with Alice Liddell and her sisters on a rowing trip upstream during which he unfolded the tale which became *Alice's Adventures in Wonderland*.

Cross the road and go ahead over the footbridge crossing the stream which runs under Grandpont House. With the winding river the towpath soon runs under Salter's crane, in front of Jubilee Terrace, and later under both a footbridge and a former railway bridge.

The **footbridge**, open to the public since 1972, was completed in 1886 to carry pipes and pedestrians between gasworks on two sides of the river. The **larger upstream bridge** carried a railway branch line into sidings at the gasworks which closed in 1958. On the far bank, immediately beyond the railway bridge, water from the Oxford canal and upstream river flows into the Thames. The river used to divide into several streams as it passed through Oxford and this stream may have been the main channel.

Round another bend there is the main line railway bridge (1850; rebuilt 1898). Bear right across the footbridge spanning Bulstrake Stream where a monument records a drowning in 1889. A millstream joins on the far bank. When the towpath crosses the weir stream to Osney Lock there is a view ahead, just behind the derelict red-brick mill, of the remains of Osney Abbey.

Beyond the lock, the way is over the weir and along the side of Osney Island, where there is the Punter pub and a line of riverside houses, to reach Osney Bridge after crossing Osney Stream. Turn right for Oxford Station.

FACILITIES INFORMATION – ABINGDON TO OXFORD

Refreshments
Abingdon: Crumbs, High Street. Open 8am–4pm (Sun 3pm).
Abingdon: The Nag's Head, Abingdon Bridge. Open all day.
Iffley Meadows: The Isis. On towpath. Apr–Aug: Thu 4pm–11pm; Fri 12–11pm;
　　Sat 10.30am–11pm; Sun 10.30am–9pm; BH Mondays 10.30am–9pm.
　　Sept–Mar: Fri–Sun only. Food 12.30–2.30 & 6.30–8.30pm (Sun 8pm).
Oxford (Folly Bridge): The Head of the River pub. Open all day in summer.

Accommodation
Abingdon: 22 East St Helen Street, OX14 5EB (01235 550979).
Abingdon: St Ethelwold's House, 30 East St Helen Street, OX14 5EB
　　(01235 555486).

Transport
Abingdon: National Rail to Oxford then Bus (www.traveline.info;
　　0871 200 2233) to Abingdon.
Oxford: National Rail.

Tourist Information
Abingdon: Old Abbey House, OX14 3JD (01235 522711).

Map
OS Explorer 170 (Abingdon) and 180 (Oxford).

STAGE 17
Oxford to Newbridge

Start   Osney Bridge, Oxford
Finish   The Rose Revived, Newbridge
Distance   13½ miles (21.7km)

This is the beginning of the more remote Thames, with only buses for public transport. Booking accommodation in advance is strongly advised. The walk out to Godstow, popular with many students and residents, passes Binsey with its treacle well. After Godstow Abbey there is the river's most northerly point, a toll bridge and miles of meadows.

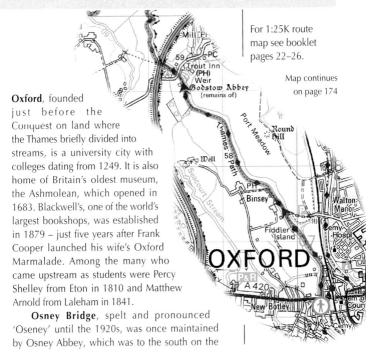

For 1:25K route map see booklet pages 22–26.

Map continues on page 174

Oxford, founded just before the Conquest on land where the Thames briefly divided into streams, is a university city with colleges dating from 1249. It is also home of Britain's oldest museum, the Ashmolean, which opened in 1683. Blackwell's, one of the world's largest bookshops, was established in 1879 – just five years after Frank Cooper launched his wife's Oxford Marmalade. Among the many who came upstream as students were Percy Shelley from Eton in 1810 and Matthew Arnold from Laleham in 1841.

Osney Bridge, spelt and pronounced 'Oseney' until the 1920s, was once maintained by Osney Abbey, which was to the south on the

173

Map continues
on page 177

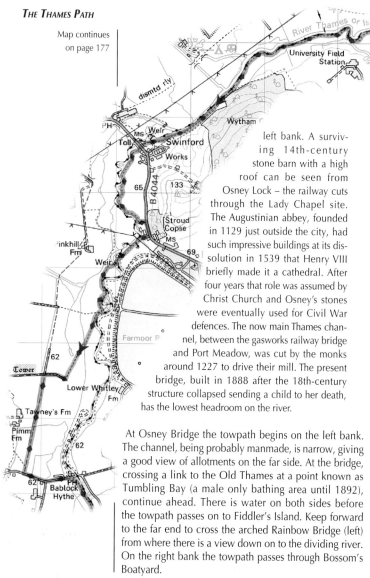

left bank. A surviving 14th-century stone barn with a high roof can be seen from Osney Lock – the railway cuts through the Lady Chapel site. The Augustinian abbey, founded in 1129 just outside the city, had such impressive buildings at its dissolution in 1539 that Henry VIII briefly made it a cathedral. After four years that role was assumed by Christ Church and Osney's stones were eventually used for Civil War defences. The now main Thames channel, between the gasworks railway bridge and Port Meadow, was cut by the monks around 1227 to drive their mill. The present bridge, built in 1888 after the 18th-century structure collapsed sending a child to her death, has the lowest headroom on the river.

At Osney Bridge the towpath begins on the left bank. The channel, being probably manmade, is narrow, giving a good view of allotments on the far side. At the bridge, crossing a link to the Old Thames at a point known as Tumbling Bay (a male only bathing area until 1892), continue ahead. There is water on both sides before the towpath passes on to Fiddler's Island. Keep forward to the far end to cross the arched Rainbow Bridge (left) from where there is a view down on to the dividing river. On the right bank the towpath passes through Bossom's Boatyard.

Bossom's Boatyard was founded in 1830 and the family includes generations of lock keepers, weir keepers and ferrymen. In 1880 Charlie Bossom towed William Morris upstream to Newbridge. The family connection here continued for another 90 years. This spot was once known as Medley Flash Lock, which was just below the bridge.

Where the now wide track strikes away from the river towards nearby Binsey is the approximate location of a ford to Port Meadow.

Binsey Ford may be the original ford of Ox-ford. Until early this century there was a ford here, once used by pilgrims to St Margaret's Well at Binsey. St Frideswide's blindness was cured at the treacle (medicinal) well, which later featured in *Alice's Adventures in Wonderland*. When restoration of the well was proposed Lewis Carroll advised 'leave well alone'.

The 342-acre grassland of **Port Meadow** was given to Oxford as a common by William the Conqueror. The ground has never been ploughed or

Port Meadow

175

built on, and rare plants flourishing include creeping marshwort and round fruited rush. Two hundred Oxford freemen and the commoners of Binsey and Wolvercote have grazing rights. The meadow's southern end floods in winter to occasionally become a popular skating rink.

Go ahead through the gate to stay by the river which bends west to pass a gate to a wooded causeway leading to Binsey's hidden Perch.

The Perch 17th-century thatched pub, which has log fires in winter, is said to be haunted by a sailor. Gerard Manley Hopkins wrote the poem *Binsey Poplars* in 1879 when he found the riverside trees felled. Their replacements between here and Godstow lasted until 2004 when the present replanting began.

After a long meadow, with no defined path, there is Godstow Lock and the ruined abbey.

Godstow means 'God's place'. The abbey was founded in 1133 by Lady Edith Launceline, who

Godstow Abbey

from Binsey saw a shaft of light touch the ground here. King Stephen was present at its consecration and it was a place of pilgrimage when the body of Rosamund de Clifford, Henry II's mistress, poisoned by Queen Eleanor, was buried here – later the body was moved. The convent buildings became ruins in the Civil War, but the abbey hospice on the far bank continues to offer hospitality as the Trout Inn, which featured in ITV's *Inspector Morse*. President Clinton visited with his student daughter Chelsea. Here on the bank Lewis Carroll's rowing party picnicked in 1862 having set out from Oxford.

Climb the bank ahead to a gate and cross the end of Godstow Bridge to continue on the towpath. Just beyond a towpath footbridge there is an Oxford City boundary marker. Pass under the A34 to the King's Lock access road, which runs direct to the lock while the towpath follows two loops on the winding river. Pass through King's Lock at the river's most northerly point. Soon there is a view ahead of Cassington church spire. The river's double bend here is known as Hagley Pool. Later, beyond the footbridge spanning the Wytham Stream, many cut the corner, but the towpath of course stays by the river. After a mile of farmland there is, near a gate, a view of the River Evenlode joining the Thames on the far bank. A little further on it is possible to look across the river and straight down Cassington Cut.

> **Cassington Cut** is a canal dug to allow barges to pass easily up to Cassington Mill ½ mile inland on the last winding stretch of the River Evenlode, which rises near Moreton-in-Marsh.

The towpath now passes through a high gate, to deter deer, to run alongside Wytham Great Wood. Later, after a second gate, keep right at a fork to cross a bridge and reach Eynsham Lock just below Swinford Bridge.

> **Swinford Bridge** was probably designed by Sir William Taylor, friend of Sir William Blackstone (see Stage 14) who masterminded the 1767 Swinford Bridge Act. In 1765 the Earl of Abingdon bought the ferry (once run by nearby Eynsham Abbey) in order to replace it and a ford (John Wesley had ridden across the year before) with the elegant bridge, completed in 1769. As the earl paid for the bridge, the Act allowed him and his successors to collect tolls tax free. Apart from a decimalisation adjustment, Parliament has approved only one toll increase – since 1994 cars are charged 5p, which is similar to the old 5d car charge based on five wheels including the spare one. Under the Act the ferry must be restored if the bridge falls down. The still privately owned bridge passed out of the Abingdon family in 1979. The Talbot pub, alongside the Wharf Stream to the north, opened in 1774.

To reach the road and bus stop at the Talbot, bear left before the bridge and go up steps. The Thames Path continues under the toll bridge and over a high footbridge. Here there is a tendency to cut a corner as the river bends – so much that it has created Horseshoe Island – to reach Oxford Cruiser Boatyard at Pinkhill. Just beyond the boatyard the towpath is lost – unchecked erosion has long left a row of houses with gardens running down to the water. Due to the missing towpath it is necessary to make a detour up to the boatyard's vehicle entrance. Go right along the road. Turn right, between Thames House and Pinkhill Lodge, down a narrow path which leads back to the towpath at a footbridge. The towpath runs to Pinkhill Lock where the Thames Path passes just outside the lock compound.

> **Pinkhill Lock**, once Pinckle Lock, dates from 1791. Today the lock marks the start of a long Thames Path diversion from the towpath in order not to rely on the ferry at Bablock Hythe.

Go right at the second gate to the Pinkhill Lock compound and walk across the upstream lock gates. Bear half left on to a grass path, passing a lamp post, and through the trees to cross the weir.

On the far side there is a kissing gate. Go half left across a large field to meet the river again beyond another kissing gate. Keep by the river to go through a kissing gate ahead and bear half right. Follow an old channel (to the left). The path joins the present navigation again at a point where the lost Skinner's Bridge crossed. Still keep ahead, as the river bends away, to reach a gate in the trees on the far side of the large field. Go through the kissing gate by this gate and bear round to the right with the track to cross a stream. Now go through the gate and bear half left across to the far corner of this smaller field. In the corner there are two gates. In winter there may be a view across the right-hand one of the church tower at Stanton Harcourt. Go through the gate ahead to continue south.

Follow the hedge on the right which gives way to a farm gate and kissing gate. Go through this gate on the right to follow a hedged road. Round the bend there is a junction.

Stanton Harcourt is one mile ahead, but the Thames Path continues left through a bridleway gate. Keep south through a series of fields to reach a lane. Turn left, and

at a junction continue forward past chalets to reach the
Ferryman Inn at Bablock Hythe Ferry.

Bablock Hythe Ferry, said to date from 950, is mentioned by Matthew Arnold in *The Scholar Gipsy*
(1853): 'Crossing the stripling Thames at Bablock-
hithe.' The ferry is operated by the Ferryman Inn,
previously called the Chequers and more recently
the Ferry Inn. A three-vehicle ferry closed in 1965.
There have been brief passenger revivals in 1981
and 1992 with a 12-seat boat.

The Thames Path rejoins the towpath (which crosses
at the ferry) by continuing right upstream through a series
of gates in the riverside meadows. Beyond a double bend,
by some ancient willows, the far bank is wooded as far
as Northmoor Lock.

(Those staying at Northmoor's Rectory Farm should
leave the river just before the gate in front of the overhead
wires. Go along the field boundary and right at the north
end for a few yards to a gate. Follow a wide path – known
as the Causeway – over several fields to a road. Turn left
for Rectory Farm next to the church.)

Despite the tread, the towpath does not cut the corner to the lock. After a mile there is Hart's Footbridge
spanning the river. Pass the bridge and later, at a bend,
there is a kissing gate leading to a track. After a very short
distance bear left on to a narrower path. Go through
gates flanking a drawdock. A short path leads to another
gate. After crossing a footbridge there is an official short
cut across a corner to a gate. Ahead is the bridge at
Newbridge flanked by two pubs. On the towpath first is
the Rose Revived.

FACILITIES INFORMATION – OXFORD TO NEWBRIDGE

Refreshments
Oxford has many cafés and pubs.
Binsey: The Perch. 10.30am–11pm.
Godstow: The Trout. 11am–11pm. Food from 12pm.
Swinford Bridge: The Talbot. Open all day. Walk past the toll gate.
Bablock Hythe: The Ferryman. Wed-Mon summer 12pm-11pm (food until
    2.30pm and after 4.30pm); Wed-Mon winter 12pm-4pm & 6.30pm-11pm
    (food until 2.30pm and after 7pm).

Accommodation
Oxford: Becket Guest House, 5 Becket Street, OX1 1PP (01865 724675).
Oxford: Sportsview Guest House, 106–110 Abingdon Road, OX1 4PX
    (01865 244268, www.sportsviewguesthouse.co.uk).
Oxford: YHA, 2a Botley Road, OX2 0AB (01865 727275, www.yha.org.uk).
Eynsham Lock: campsite (01865 881324).
Swinford Bridge: The Talbot OX8 1BT (01865 881348). Walk past the toll gate.
Bablock Hythe: The Ferryman, OX8 1BL (01865 880028). Also campsite.
Northmoor: Rectory Farm, OX8 4PX (01865 300207). Feb–Nov, Sun–Thu.
    16th-century farmhouse, once belonging to St John's College Oxford, now
    in hands of third generation of Florey family. Picnic lunches if notice given
    (www.oxtowns.co.uk/rectoryfarm).

Transport
Oxford: National Rail.
Swinford Bridge: Bus (www.traveline.info; 0871 200 2233).
Newbridge: Bus (www.traveline.info; 0871 200 2233).

Tourist Information
Oxford: 15–16 Broad Street, OX1 3AS (01865 686430,
    www.visitoxfordandoxfordshire.com).

Map
OS Explorer 180 (Oxford).

STAGE 18

Newbridge to Lechlade

Start	The Rose Revived, Newbridge
Finish	Halfpenny Bridge, Lechlade
Distance	16 miles (25.7km)

The Thames here is unspoilt but can also be lonely. As recently as the 1980s the towpath between Tenfoot Bridge and Tadpole was impenetrable. The approach to Lechlade is past William Morris's Kelmscott Manor, where Compton Mackenzie wrote 'on this stile Swinburne may have sat; there Burne-Jones may have looked back at the sky; and ... Rosetti tied up his shoe ...'. Booking accommodation ahead is again advised, although at Lechlade there is more choice.

For 1:25K route map see booklet pages 14–22.

Newbridge, the second oldest bridge on the river, is 'new' because it was built after Radcot Bridge. Newbridge, with six pointed medieval arches and dating from around 1250, was built by Benedictines from St Denis near Paris who were living at nearby Northmoor. They placed the bridge in the care of a hermit whose tollhouse on the south side has become the Maybush. The builders used Taynton Quarry stone, brought here on the River Windrush which joins on the north upstream side. Four hundred years later

Map continues on page 185

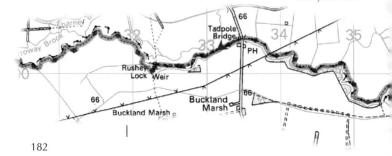

Wren had Taynton stone floated down to London for St Paul's Cathedral. Earlier this bridge had been the scene of two Civil War skirmishes. The Rose Revived on the north side until recently had a sign, painted in 1919 by Alfred Parsons RA, showing roses being revived with Morland's ale.

Cross the bridge from the Rose Revived to turn down the side of the Maybush. Go through the TC gate at the foot-bridge. A causeway takes the towpath towards the river. After several gates the path runs below a slope. At the river bend there is a gated footbridge leading to a meadow.

Haul Ham is a meadow which was once an island. Behind is Harrowdown Hill where scientist Dr David Kelly was found dead in 2003. His nearby house had been the home of poet Wilfred Howe-Nurse who in 1927 wrote: 'On Harrowdown the golden gorse now flames,/While in rich meadows set with many flowers/The cattle graze beside the silver Thames/Or seek its shallows cool in sunny hours.'

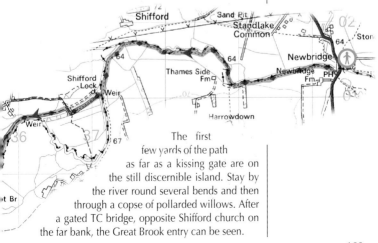

The first few yards of the path as far as a kissing gate are on the still discernible island. Stay by the river round several bends and then through a copse of pollarded willows. After a gated TC bridge, opposite Shifford church on the far bank, the Great Brook entry can be seen.

Towpath trees opposite Shifford

King Alfred is said to have held the first meeting of an English 'parliament' at **Shifford** in 890. The community has declined, leaving a farm and a church, rebuilt in 1863. There was a flash lock here before Shifford Lock was built upstream. The Great Brook was dug in the mid 19th century as an irrigation channel stretching back 2½ miles towards Bampton.

The path continues alongside a field and before the end there is a view of Shifford Lock. Cross the bridge leading to Shifford Island and Cut.

Shifford Lock Cut opened in 1897 after a year's work which created an island. The idea was not just to avoid a 1¼ mile loop and save ¾ mile, but to remove a twisting and shallow navigation which was forcing barge traffic to turn back at Newbridge. The footbridge crossing, replacing a lost ferry across the Old Thames to the lock, opened in 1994 in advance of the proposed Thames Path route. The old towpath continues by the Old Thames to the ford at Duxford, but walkers are warned that crossing the ford can be dangerous, especially when the river is running high in winter.

Follow the path along the north side of Shifford island. Across the weir stream there is a view of Shifford Lock before the path follows the cut. A gate ahead leads to a bridleway. (Go left only for Duxford.) The Thames Path continues to the right over the Cut. At once go left through a gate and down steps to rejoin the towpath. At the end of the cut there is a view of a weir at the entrance to the Old Thames flowing down to Duxford.

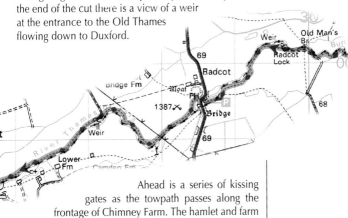

Ahead is a series of kissing gates as the towpath passes along the frontage of Chimney Farm. The hamlet and farm buildings can be seen inland.

Chimney Meadows riverside

Chimney Farm, purchased in 2003 by the Berkshire, Buckinghamshire and Oxfordshire Wildlife Trust, belonged to the Church Commissioners until 1921, but continued to be farmed by the Gauntlett family, who had arrived at the end of the 19th century, until 1994. West of the farm buildings is Chimney Meadows, one of England's largest areas of unimproved meadows and rich in wildflowers. 'Chimney' comes from 'Ceomma's Island', reflecting the marshy area.

Later the towpath is briefly away from the water as it cuts a corner in the meadows. Shortly afterwards the path passes Tenfoot Bridge.

Tenfoot Bridge dates from 1869, when the bridge replaced a weir which had a 10ft gap for navigation.

Here there is a short tunnel of trees. The river winds and the towpath, running along the top of a floodbank, tends to be narrow with an occasional TC gate often set back from the riverside. Inland there are meadows and opposite the bank is wooded. Eventually Tadpole Bridge can be seen ahead. The path runs up to a gate on the bridge.

Tadpole Bridge was probably built in 1789. The 17th-century Trout Inn on the right bank was until 1875 separated from the bridge by a toll gate. The first mention of the name Tadpole is on a 1761 map where the spelling is 'Tadpoll'. From 1791 until 1914 there was a wharf here for Bampton 1½ miles to the north.

The towpath continues ahead through a gate to join a metalled road which runs for a mile to Rushey Lock. Go through the gate to cross the lower lock gates. Go right to pass the hut and then left down the side of the cottage. Cross the weir and at once turn right to a gate. The towpath is now by meadows and briefly under old willows. There are tempting but confusing unofficial short cuts at the many river bends.

Paddles at Rushey Lock weir

From Old Man's Bridge the way is metalled as far as nearby Radcot Lock. At the far end of the compound a long grass path leads to a TC gate. Later, after a sharp bend southwards opposite a backwater entrance, the towpath crosses Cradle Bridge spanning the Old Thames. Follow the new channel to Radcot Bridge. The Swan is on the far bank.

There has been a bridge at **Radcot** since 958. The Earl of Oxford had leapt over a gap here on his horse when fleeing from battle in 1387, so the present medieval bridge across the Old Thames probably dates from 1393, with work undertaken by Normandy monks who lived at Faringdon. The downstream parapet has a niche for a statue which May Morris (daughter of William) in a sketch filled with a figure of the Virgin Mary. She saved the bridge from falling into dangerous disrepair with a vigorous campaign just before the First World War. Navigation is under a new bridge built in 1787 when a backstream was enlarged to cope with traffic using the Thames and Severn Canal. Radcot House to the north is 17th-century. The farmland on the left downstream bank belongs to the moated Friars Court Farm on the site of a Knights Hospitaller preceptory. The Swan is a late 17th-century building with a log fire in winter.

Cross the navigation channel bridge to find the towpath continuing on the left beyond a gate. The river runs southwest and northwest to curve round to Grafton Lock. After a riverside pillbox there is are double gates and an early view through trees of Eaton Hastings and its church on the far bank.

Eaton Hastings church is partly Norman. 'Hastings' comes from Ralph de Hastings who owned the village in the 12th century.

On passing through a gate by a pillbox it is possible to see (half right) the chimneys of Kelmscott Manor. After a double bend there is a kissing gate where the towpath becomes a track leading to Kelmscott.

Artist and manufacturer William Morris, who first saw **Kelmscott** from the river approach, lived at Kelmscott Manor from 1871 until his death in 1896 at Hammersmith. He described this house as 'heaven on earth' and walked the riverbank collecting reeds, grasses and flowers for dyes and patterns for textiles. When the meadows flooded the post was delivered by punt and the Morris family would cross the grass in a flat-bottomed boat. His utopian story *News From Nowhere* ends with travellers arriving at Kelmscott. Morris is buried in the churchyard of the partly Norman church which he helped to 'preserve' rather than 'restore'. The spirit of Morris lives on, with even the village hall designed by Morris disciple Ernest Gimson and opened by Bernard Shaw. The Manor, in the hands of the Society of Antiquaries, is open on the first Wed, Apr–Sep, 11am–5pm; admission charge.

Before reaching the village buildings, cross the gated footbridge into a field to follow the towpath to a wood by Eaton Footbridge crossing.

There was a **flash lock** here known as Hart's Weir after a family who supplied the lock keepers for generations. The Anchor Inn, on the right bank, was burnt down in 1980. Beyond the bridge there is the last TC gate.

Keep past the bridge to the TC gate leading to a field. Gloucestershire is reached at the far end of the field. Afterwards the path is clear as the river enjoys several bends. Later the towpath crosses a bridge on to an island to reach Buscot Lock.

Buscot village has a well, hall and houses built by the first Lord Faringdon of nearby 18th-century

Buscot Park. In the mid 20th century the second Lord Faringdon hosted Fabian Society gatherings there and added Labour heritage murals. The riverside Cotswold stone Old Parsonage was built in 1703 alongside the church, which has a 15th-century tower and two Burne-Jones windows. The right bank upstream of the lock was known as Brandy Island when from 1869 to 1879 Robert Campbell, who preceded Lord Faringdon at Buscot Park, set up the Berkshire Distillery and exported the alcohol to France by river via London. A tramway ran to now-landlocked Buscot Wharf which was connected to the Thames by a canal. A little upstream of the riverside parsonage is a spot called Cheese Wharf, where Gloucester cheeses were landed from small craft to be loaded into barges for London.

The towpath continues, not across the lock gates, but over the weir bridge to the right. Bear left along the edge of the huge meadow. At a bend there is a fine view of Buscot church and the Old Parsonage with two busts on the wall. There are three bends, with views of Lechlade church spire, before the path reaches Bloomer's Hole where the towpath switches banks.

The origin of the name **Bloomer's Hole** is obscure, although 'hole' means 'place where water is deep' and is often a turning point. The stepped wooden bridge, which arrived here by helicopter in 2001, is on the line of an old ferry.

Cross the bridge, and after a short distance there is a footbridge and later a gate before the towpath passes under St John's Bridge to reach St John's Lock.

A series of wooden bridges at today's **St John's Lock** was replaced by a stone crossing in 1229, and soon after the Priory of St John was built on the left bank with the monks maintaining the bridge. The Trout, formerly the St John the Baptist's Head, was opened

Lechlade from St John's Lock

as a inn by the monks in 1472. Three years later Edward IV dissolved the seven-strong community, but left one priest in charge of the bridge. The pub has inherited the priory's fishing rights. During the Civil War General Fairfax rode over from the south with troops ready to rout the Lechlade Royalists. The present bridge was erected in 1886. The lock, opened in 1790 and rebuilt in 1905, is the last and highest on the river. In 1830 the lock keeper was also running the Trout. The lock's 'Old Father Thames', made for the 1851 Great Exhibition, stood at the Source from 1958 to 1974.

Go through the gate at the end of the lock compound, and after a short distance cross a footbridge (which spanned a now-diverted spur of the River Cole) marking the boundary between Oxfordshire (Old Berkshire) and Wiltshire. After a further short distance there is a gate next to the last TC stile, identified by the remaining blue-grey paint that can be seen on its upstream side. Stay by the winding river with the Lechlade spire always in view. On approaching Lechlade's Halfpenny Bridge there is a clear view across to the sweeping lawns and archway of the New Inn in Lechlade. Go through the gates on each side of the towpath tunnel under Halfpenny Bridge. Steps on the left lead up onto the bridge and the road running into Lechlade.

FACILITIES INFORMATION – NEWBRIDGE TO LECHLADE

Refreshments
Newbridge: The Rose Revived. Open all day.
Tadpole: The Trout. Mon–Fri 11.30am-3pm and 6pm–11pm;
    Sat 11.30am–11pm; Sun 12pm–10.30pm. Teas weekend afternoons.
Radcot: The Swan. Mon–Fri 12pm–3pm and 5pm–11pm; weekends all day.
Kelmscott: The Plough. 11.30am–midnight. Food 12pm–2.30pm and
    6pm–9pm; Sun all day.
St John's Bridge: The Trout. Mon–Sat 12–11pm; Sun 12–9pm. Food 12–2pm
    and 7pm–9.30pm (Sun 8.30pm).

Accommodation
Newbridge: The Rose Revived, OX29 7QD. (01865 300221).
Tadpole: The Trout Inn, Tadpole Bridge, SN7 8RD (01367 870382,
    www.trout-inn.co.uk).
Rushey Lock campsite: (01367 870218). Apr-Oct.
Kelmscott: The Plough, GL7 3HG (01367 253543,
    www.theploughinnkelmscott.com). 17th-century inn.

Transport
Newbridge: Bus (www.traveline.info; 0871 200 2233).
Lechlade: Bus (www.traveline.info; 0871 200 2233) to Swindon then
    National Rail.

Tourist Information
Oxford: 15–16 Broad Street, OX1 3AS (01865 686430,
    www.visitoxfordandoxfordshire.com).

Maps
OS Explorer 170 (Abingdon) and 180 (Oxford).

STAGE 19

Lechlade to Cricklade

Start	Halfpenny Bridge, Lechlade
Finish	Cricklade High Street
Distance	10½ miles (16.8km)

Soon after Lechlade the towpath ends and, although navigation is technically allowed as far as Cricklade, only canoes now make it any further upstream as the river is narrow and shallow. In the 1850s it was often full of tall reeds, but was cleared by the 1870s, which allowed for about 3ft of water for some navigation. For today's walkers there is one long diversion on a main road until a new riverside path, extending the towpath, is created. **Note** With increased traffic walkers are advised to avoid road walking by calling a taxi (01367 252575/253424) or stopping a Swindon bus.

For 1:25K route map see booklet pages 9–14.

Lechlade is mentioned in the Domesday Book. Its landmark church has been described as one of the six best in Gloucestershire. The perfect perpendicular building dates from 1476 and may have been

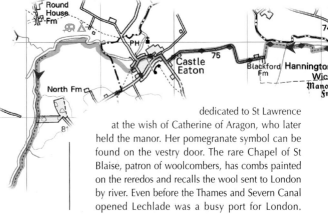

dedicated to St Lawrence at the wish of Catherine of Aragon, who later held the manor. Her pomegranate symbol can be found on the vestry door. The rare Chapel of St Blaise, patron of woolcombers, has combs painted on the reredos and recalls the wool sent to London by river. Even before the Thames and Severn Canal opened Lechlade was a busy port for London.

Map continues on page 197

The very early 18th-century Church House in the churchyard was built by John Aing, who ran a wharf behind for landing London goods. The garden has a fine gazebo seen from Shelley Walk, which recalls the poet's visit in 1815, when he stayed two nights at the New Inn and wrote *A Summer-evening Churchyard, Lechlade*. Later Compton Mackenzie featured the town as 'Ladingford' in his novel *Guy and Pauline*, writing 'the spire of the church remained so long in sight'.

Until **Halfpenny Bridge** was completed in 1793 most traffic had to use St John's Bridge, as only pedestrians could use a ferry at the end of Bell Lane. This bridge was made high to avoid the need to lower masts on all the new barges passing under from the new Thames and Severn Canal. The stones of the arch are arranged radially, as with the first Westminster Bridge which had just been built.

The tollhouse remains, although the bridge has been toll free since 1875. The ½d toll that gave the crossing its name was levied on walkers (except church goers and mourners) until 1839.

Halfpenny Bridge at Lechlade

On the south upstream side, steps lead down to the towpath. Continue upstream and from the towpath there is a view over to the last boatyard on the river. Cross a footbridge (over a braid) to leave Wiltshire and enter Gloucestershire for a short period. Soon there is the last bridge over the navigable Thames. A few yards further on is the footing of the now lost footbridge which carried the towpath over the river to continue along the canal which began by the Round House opposite.

The Round House marks the end of navigation on the Thames, which flows to the left of the building. To the right is the former entrance to the Thames and Severn Canal, which from 1789 took navigation on beyond the source to join the Stroudwater Navigation. Suddenly salt from Droitwich and fruit from Evesham was taken down the Thames to London. Percy and Mary Shelley, Charles Clairmont and Thomas Love Peacock arrived here in a rowing boat in September 1815 intending to go up the canal, but found the £20 toll too steep. Instead they continued on the river towards Inglesham church, but when the reeds became too thick and the water too shallow they stopped rowing and allowed the flow to carry them back towards Halfpenny Bridge. Canal traffic was eventually reduced by the arrival of the railways which even reached Lechlade. The waterway was abandoned in 1933, but now the Stroudwater and Severn Canal Trust is engaged on a long restoration programme.

Continue by the Thames as it double bends to Murdock Ditch (once a significant braid) on the Gloucestershire–Wiltshire boundary. Cross a footbridge (which is now a little inland) to re-enter Wiltshire. From here head across a field towards the left side of the buildings at Inglesham. A gate leads to a road. The church is to the right just beyond Inglesham House.

Inglesham is the site of a lost village where only a 13th-century church and a farm remain. The redundant church on a mound was saved from over-restoration in the 19th century by William Morris, who loved its old simplicity and box pews. There are wall paintings and a Virgin and Child carving on the south wall.

There is no riverside path, so the Thames Path continues to the left from the stile to reach a T-junction at the main road. Go right along the main road for just over a mile, crossing the River Cole, to Upper Inglesham. (The verge on the left may prove better than being on the right facing on-coming traffic, but see introduction on page 194.)

At Upper Inglesham go right (opposite Lynt Farm Lane) to pass Middle Hill Farm on the corner and the

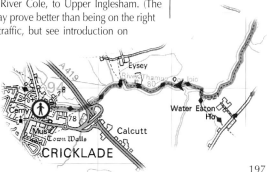

Forge Restaurant. (Littleholme is the former YHA hostel.) At the bend go through a gate on the right on to a bridleway. The path runs straight ahead up the side of a long field. There may be several gates on the way linked sometimes to temporary fencing. A final view (right) of Lechlade church is possible just before the path bears round to the left to ford a stream. (There is a footbridge to the left.) Go through the gate and along the right side of a field. Where the hedge ends, continue ahead across an open field. The path double bends at the Sterts Farm boundary. Stay by the stream in the ditch on the right After ¾ mile there is a gate, and the way soon meets a metalled road by a house. Turn left to a junction. Ahead is Hannington Wick, but the Thames Path continues to the right to pass Bridge Cottage and Farm. Go left just before the first Hannington Bridge.

> **Hannington Bridge**, built in the early 1840s on the line of a Roman crossing, spans a (sometimes dry) braid of the Thames as well as the main channel with its left bank in Gloucestershire.

Go through the gateway on the left and walk along the side of three fields with the river braid to the right. At the corner of the third field there is a gate and footbridge. Continue alongside the river braid, passing a ford, to another footbridge at a point where the channel and river meet. There are now the best views of Kempsford's church tower.

> **Kempsford** was a detached part of the Duchy of Lancaster. The landmark church tower was built in 1390 by John of Gaunt, Duke of Lancaster, in memory of his wife who had died in 1369. Behind the village is Fairford airbase, used by the US Air Force for many years, including wartime, and for testing Concorde.

At the field corner do not be tempted ahead with the river, but bear left with the hedge and at a gap turn right to find Blackford Farm at the start of Blackford Lane. Follow the road round two bends to reach Castle Eaton. Turn right to bear left into School Lane and go right up Long Row to the start of the Street. Opposite is the lychgate entrance to a long path up to the church. Continue along the Street to reach the Red Lion and the turning to the bridge.

> The site of the castle at **Castle Easton** is unknown, but near the church there was a manor house which was turned into a fortress in 1311. The riverside church has Norman doorways, and above its 13th-century chancel is a bell turret with the original 13th-century sanctus bell, found and rehung in 1900. The present bell turret was added by William Butterfield when he undertook restoration in 1861, having just completed his work on the new St Alban's Holborn. In the nearby riverside Red Lion, a Georgian inn describing itself as 'the first pub on the Thames', there is a picture of the earlier bridge here, which has been replaced by the iron structure.

At the west end of the Street keep ahead along Mill Lane. After the last house continue down the slope and over the gated bridge.

There is a pond on the right. After a few yards bear right towards the river, passing a clump of trees hiding a pond on the left. At the river turn left upstream. After a footbridge, the river takes a long S-bend to give a view of an old Thames-side chalet at a campsite on the far bank.

There is another footbridge and a more gentle bend before reaching a band of trees. Do not be tempted south away from the river but take a narrow path through the young trees to find a footbridge.

There is then open country, apart from a high long bridge over an inlet, as the path runs near the Water Eaton farm buildings. Here there is a first view ahead of St Sampson's church tower at Cricklade. The path bears right with the Thames to a bridge spanning the river.

Cross the river footbridge and turn left upstream with the path. Shortly, the River Ray joins from the far side.

Cricklade's landmark tower

Soon the way is up a slope and behind riverside trees. As the ground drops, bear left to a gate to stay by the river. Up on the hill (right) is a wooded enclosure. On reaching another river bridge cross back to the opposite bank. (The bridge's stiles had a lifting top bar.) Turn right. Soon, Down Ampney Brook flows into the Thames from the north side – there was a ford here in the last century. After a gate, and beyond a pipe bridge, there is a foot-bridge over a ditch – this was the mouth of the tiny River Key until the bypass was built in 1975. Go under the new road and through a gate into a field to find Cricklade's young Millennium Wood. After a short distance go right over a bridge spanning the diverted River Key. Walk ahead alongside a playing field towards Cricklade with the Thames on the right. Enter a second field to cross the stone stile in the right-hand corner. Cross open ground (a former farm) to a lane. To the right is Hatchetts Ford, but the Thames Path runs to the left up Thames Lane and right into Abingdon Court Lane to reach Cricklade High Street.

FACILITIES INFORMATION – LECHLADE TO CRICKLADE

Refreshments
Lechlade: The Riverside, next to Halfpenny Bridge. Open all day.
Lechlade: The Crown, High Street. Open all day.
Lechlade: The Black Cat Restaurant and Tea Rooms, High Street. Open daily to 4.30pm.
Castle Eaton: The Red Lion, The Street. Open all day Fri–Sun, Mon–Thu lunchtimes and weekday evenings from 6pm. Riverside garden.

Accommodation
Lechlade: Cambrai Lodge, Oak St, GL7 3AY (01367 253173).
Lechlade: The New Inn, Market Square, GL7 3AB (01367 252296, www.newinnhotel.com).
Lechlade: Bridge House campsite, GL7 3AG (01367 252348). Apr–Oct.
Castle Eaton: The Malt House, The Street, SN6 6JZ (01285 810822).
Castle Eaton: The Red Lion, The Street, SN6 6JZ (01285 810280).

Transport
Lechlade: National Rail to Swindon then bus (www.traveline.info; 0871 200 2233).
Cricklade: Bus 51 (www.traveline.info; 0871 200 2233) to Swindon then National Rail.

Tourist Information
Swindon: Central Library, Regent Circus, SN1 1QG (01793 530328).

Map
OS Explorer 169 (Cirencester and Swindon) and 170 (Abingdon).

STAGE 20

Cricklade to the Source

Start   Town Bridge, Cricklade
Finish   Thames Source Stone (ST 979 996)
Distance 12¼ miles (19.7km)

In the early 20th century there were people who could remember the Thames being open for barges as far as Waterhay Bridge, due to the riverbed having being dragged by horses in a dry summer. This final section involves a diversion around lakes in the Cotswold Water Park before Waterhay is reached. Here the river changes dramatically in size and scenery for the final few miles. The Source is a lonely spot, but there is a handy station nearby.

Map continues on page 204

Cricklade means 'place by the river crossing', and the town motto, 'in lovely surroundings', is derived from a 12th-century document. Cricklade lies on a kink of the Roman-built Ermin Street and has been described as an example of a Saxon new town. The landmark tower on St Sampson's Church was added by Lady Jane Grey's father-in-law just before his execution. Inside the tower is the Westminster Abbey shield (it held the church in Norman times), and mysteriously the

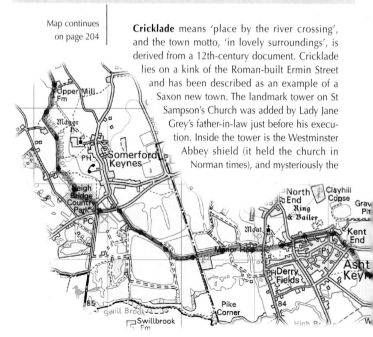

spade, heart, diamond and club of the playing card which led William Morris to suggest that the tower was paid for by a successful gamble. Near Town Bridge is the older St Mary's, which has a Norman chancel arch, and since 1983 is again a Roman Catholic church, making it 'Britain's oldest Roman Catholic church'. In 1821 William Cobbett described Cricklade as a 'villainous hole' due to its poverty. Then, the Bath Road at the side of

St Mary's Church at Cricklade

For 1:25K route map see booklet pages 4–9.

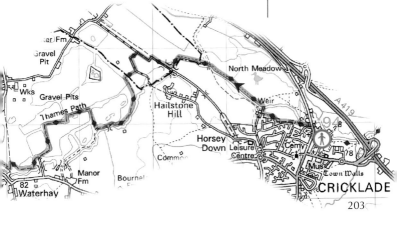

the Vale was the main road, making the junction a crossroads. The market cross had already been moved to the churchyard, but now the 1897 Jubilee Clock is the focal point at the junction. The wide main street sloping down to the Thames had a monthly cattle market until 1944. The White Hart, dating from at least James I's reign, was rebuilt in 1890. Hatchetts Ford at the end of Thames Lane was the scene of Baptist baptisms into the early 20th century – in the Victorian era there was also the wooden Plank Bridge on the downstream side.

The first town bridge was built by the Romans, who created the long causeway from the town, crossing not only the Thames but also the River Churn and the water meadows. From above this bridge the river ceases to be open to craft. From Roman times until the 1830s there was a wharf on the east side of the road stretching south to just beyond the present war memorial. The bridge was rebuilt in 1854 to include, in the corner of

the bus stop wait-ing area, steps (now gone) down to a 'watergate' where water could be drawn

– an iron fence below protected children from falling into the river. Riverside, to the north, is the site of a tanyard, and next door St John's Priory gave shelter and food to passersby from at least 1231 until the 1530s. The outline of the chapel window can be seen from the road.

At the north end of the High Street do not cross Town Bridge but go left along North Wall. Walk on the right near the Thames to leave the road after a short distance and go through a gate into a field. Keep forward, and as the river swings away go to another gate into a large meadow. Continue forward near the left-hand side of the meadow to find ahead a gap under a tree on the far side. Go ahead with houses to the left and after a very short distance go through the kissing gate to the right.

Bear half left across the grass to a gate. Follow a fenced path and at a willow go right over a railway sleeper footbridge. Turn right through a gate and bear left round a shed on the site of West Mill to cross the river on a wide concrete bridge.

West Mill stood here from at least 1300 until demolished by Thames Conservancy in 1938. The rebuilt weir is an Environment Agency gauging weir measuring the quantity of water coming down. The mill took over the work of Town Mill which for a time was a few yards upstream from Town Bridge.

Once across the River Thames turn left through a gate and follow the river. At the third field, a gate leads to North Meadow.

Centuries of regular hay cutting and grazing have caused this **field**, filled with colourful flowers, to become one of the finest uncultivated ancient meadows in Britain. Plants found include adder's tongue, great burnet, marsh marigold, water crowfoot, buttercup, celandine and the largest number anywhere of the rare snake's head (or fritillary) flowering in late spring. Most of the fritillaries are purple, although in the last 30 years there has been an increase in the number of white flowers. Once, all the flowers were picked for local use or sent to Covent Garden, but now picking is forbidden and visitors must keep to the public footpaths. Cutting of the organic hay begins on 1 July and, although most of the land is now owned by English Nature, different people – some using scythes – cut the old allotment areas as marked by the stones. On 12 August (Lammas Day in the old calendar) the Hayward (appointed by the Cricklade Court Leet) unpadlocks the gate to allow cattle to graze – until recently they were herded down Cricklade's main street and along the causeway. Horses go on in September, sheep take over in winter and, unless there is flooding from the Thames, stay until 12 February (Candlemas Eve in the old calendar).

Shortly before approaching the old canal crossing there is, by the water, one of the meadow allotment stones. Steps lead up to a gate on the bridge.

Old Canal Bridge, now rebuilt for a bridleway, was once a canal bridge taking the Latton–Swindon Canal, built in 1819 as a branch of the Thames and Severn Canal, across the Thames. The bed of the canal can be seen running north.

Do not cross the Thames, but go through the gate (right) to continue down a slope and along the winding bank with the water to the left. There is a view back to the Cricklade church tower before the end of the field. Keep forward to join a track as the Thames bears left, curving south round Hailstone Hill to a former railway bridge.

Hailstone Hill, once Holy Stone Hill, had a chapel dedicated to St Helen. The hill was cut through by the Swindon–Cirencester railway line which opened in 1883. The track was lifted in 1964 and now forms a short section of the Thames Path.

Do not go under the bridge, but follow the track up to the farm gate where there is a another gate. Once on the former railway embankment go right through a gate and walk ahead on the wide straight path which is part of the Cotswold Water Park.

Extensive quarrying for sand and gravel through the 20th century has left over 133 lakes covering over 40 square miles which now make up the **water park**. Several lakes are given over to wildlife.

Soon there is a signpost pointing left to 'Ashton Keynes 3 miles'. Here, go left on the bridleway, which bears right and bends twice more before reaching the second turning on the right. Go right and stay on this path which soon crosses a footbridge and bears left near Cleveland Lakes. As this way bends the Thames comes into view on the left. After Bournelake Farm bridge the way divides. Pass the left-hand gate marked 'No access' and take the right fork which runs north, west (left) to a gate and along the top of Manorbrook Lake. The lakeside path bends three times before reaching a gate. Follow the enclosed path to a junction near Waterhay Bridge. Go left for a short distance to find a gap on the right.

Diversion to visit Waterhay Bridge
Here only continue ahead to visit Waterhay Bridge. Walk through the car park to the road and turn left.)

The water flowing under the **bridge** is now recognised as the Thames, although the main flow here is from the Swill Brook swollen by a couple of Thames braids. The imbalance is largely due to considerable changes in drainage patterns caused by the gravel extraction which has reduced the Thames flow from Kemble. The bridge takes its name from a village to the south which has largely disappeared.

The infant Thames near Waterhay

So reduced was the population by 1896 that all but the 13th-century chancel of All Saints Church was moved to nearby Leigh and rededicated as St Leonard's.

Beyond the gap, a once important Thames braid is to the left for a short distance. This area, still fields in the 1980s, was ruined in the early 1990s when gravel extraction tore out the hedges and obliterated the stream, which ceased to enjoy a continuous flow along its historic channel. The path now passes between two lakes. After ½ mile there is an old Thames bridge (left), but the river water here now flows into the lake. The Thames Path goes ahead through a kissing gate to pass through a millennium green. On the far side a gate leads to a playing field. Walk in front of the pavilion to a kissing gate in front of the house. Cross the driveway to another gate at Rixon End on the edge of Ashton Keynes.

Ashton Keynes was described by William Cobbett in 1826 as 'a very curious place'. Here, like Oxford, the Thames briefly divided into several channels, but now the western flow alongside the High Road is considered to be the main Thames. The village has four crosses (all damaged by Roundheads) and their origin is still a mystery. The one in the churchyard became the war memorial in 1917. The church, dating from Saxon times and appropriately dedicated to the Holy Cross, was restored in 1876–7 by Butterfield, who enlarged the Norman chancel arch. Nextdoor Church Farm has a house with a moat fed by the Thames. Keynes is derived from the de Kaines family who arrived with William the Conqueror and became local landowners.

Go left for a few yards, and then right down a waymarked path by the Rixon Gate sign. Soon there is Bourne Cottage to the left. When the path turns sharp left to a stone footbridge do not cross the river but go right through a kissing gate. Follow the fenced path alongside a field. After another kissing gate go left over the stream and follow a lane with the water to the right.

At the T-junction, where the stream disappears down the side of Bridge Cottage (ahead), the Thames Path turns right to follow Back Street along the back of the village.

Ashton Keynes

209

(To reach the village post office and shop go left and right into Fore Street.) At the end of Back Street turn left into High Road to cross Gumstool Bridge over the Thames, which flows both down the side of a thatched cottage and south by the High Road. (Keep ahead only for the pubs.)

Turn right by the cross to go up Church Walk alongside the now wider river. The Thames Path is ahead where the river emerges from a narrow mill race. Beyond the corn mill passage the path is beside a field and the river begins to take on the nature of a canal. Some distance after a gate there is a view of Church Farm's moat entry.

Cross the road and continue ahead with a lake to the left. The path crosses a weir which sends water down to Swill Brook by way of a wood known as Flood Hatches Copse. The river does a gentle double bend before passing a track crossing and a footbridge. The way crosses the Wiltshire–Gloucestershire boundary at the end of Freeth's Wood where there is a gate. On the left there is Lower Mill Lake. At the second bridge, the path switches bank to run past Lower Mill Estate where the wide way becomes a metalled road.

> **Lower Mill Estate**, by the flooded gravel extraction pit, was created in the 1990s around the buildings of Lower Mill Farm. The mill was grinding cattle feed for local farms until the 1960s. The piggery is now the shop for the holiday home waterside village.

The river and the millstream is lost from view near the main road. At the junction cross the main road and go left past a lane running into Somerford Keynes.

> **Somerford** means 'a place where the river can be crossed in summer' and Keynes refers to the family of nearby downstream Ashton Keynes. The church, founded in 685 on land given by the King of Mercia to St Aldhelm, has a Saxon doorway on the south side. The next-door Manor House, shored up with

buttresses when a floor was added in the 17th century, has a dovecot. The Baker's Arms dates from the 16th century.

Cross the river and go right at a crossroads into Neigh Bridge (road). Beyond the entrance to Neigh Bridge Country Park and before the bridge go left to rejoin the river. Follow the winding Thames riverbank. To the left there is the last of the many lakes. At the end of the lake, cross the Thames on a footbridge and stay on the left near the infant river. After a kissing gate the path passes the partly 16th-century Kemble Mill.

Over to the right is Somerford Keynes church and Manor House. The path continues along the hedge (masking the river) to another kissing gate. Keep forward by the water, crossing a bridge set back at an inlet. Go through a kissing gate to pass Old Mill Farm. The path, indicated by a couple of waymark posts, is away from the riverbank to skirt an often dry pond before swinging left back to the river after the farm. Keep by the fence (left) and do not be tempted over the footbridge. Later the path crosses a footbridge over a stream feeding the Thames (left) to enter a field which has a windpump in the centre.

The path runs with the river and then a millstream to a footbridge just before Upper Mill Farm. Cross the mill race and turn right upstream to pass the house. Beyond a kissing gate leading to a field there is a view of Kemble's church spire to the left. The path now stays beside the river as far as Ewen. On the way there are a couple of gates, a winding stretch (ignore the gate ahead) and a young wood beyond a kissing gate. The path passes in front of Brookside, an attractive house with a gazebo, before reaching a gate at the road. Go right over the bridge leaving the river to flow alone. The lane passes the front of Brookside at the bend before reaching a T-junction in Ewen. The pub is to the right; left fork.

Ewen means 'source of a river'. The Source is still some distance away, but Mill Farm at the west end had the last (or first) mill on the river – the water table has only fallen in modern times with gravel and water extraction. The village had a chapel until it was taken down to provide the south chapel of the restored Kemble church in 1877. Ewen Manor is Georgian.

The Thames Path continues to the left along the road. Just past Mill Farm, and by the village sign, continue behind the hedge on the left to find the Thames joining to the left. The WI has placed a seat here for 'Thameswalkers'. When the path returns to the road go left for a few yards to Parker's Bridge. Do not cross the river but turn right down a step to follow the river. Round a bend, beyond a barn, there is a gate set back from the river to pass through. Stay by the river (with some young trees to the right) to reach the Kemble–Cirencester road on the edge of Kemble (left).

Kemble is a quiet village with an outstanding Brunel railway station, built when this was a junction with a line to Cirencester. The local landmark is the church's stone spire resting on a 13th-century tower. The Tavern Inn was the station's Coffee Tavern refreshment rooms until 1946.

At the road, cross over and bear right to find that the river has crossed at an angle. Go over the stile by the bridge. After a short distance cross a footbridge over a (usually dry) tributary.

To reach Kemble Station
Go right. Follow a slightly raised path by the old railway embankment (left) to a stile and continue to a second stile at a road. Turn left to go uphill and right into the station approach.

The Thames Path follows the riverbank for about 200 yards to a lonely tree. Here bear half left away from the water to walk close to the hedge over to the left. Go over the stiles at the concrete farm road. Continue ahead on high ground by the hedge. On coming level with a solitary house (over to the right), curve round to the right to join the shallow indentation of the tiny Thames, which is usually dry by now. Head for a telegraph pole to find steps leading up to the road. On the right is the tunnel for the infant Thames.

> The high-up main road is the Roman-built Cirencester–Bath Foss Way. **Thames Head Bridge**, 200 yards east, carries the road over the former Thames and Severn Canal, next to Thames Head Wharf where barges from London were unloaded.

Cross the main Cirencester road to a gap almost opposite and go up to a gate set back from the road. Climb over the stile on the right to reach the far side of the gate and follow the side of the field. The Thames valley is to the right. At the far end of the field go through the squeeze stile by a gate. The stone wall to the right of the gate is built to allow water to flow underneath when the Thames is in flood. Ahead can be seen the tower of Coates church. Follow the line of trees (right) up the valley to a stile by a gate. Bear half right to find, under an ash tree, a stone marking the source of the Thames.

> The **source** is marked by a simple stone placed here in 1974 by the Conservators of the River Thames, who that year became part of the Thames Water Authority. 'Old Father Thames', now at St John's Lock, stood here from 1958 to 1974. Although the source usually appears dry there is of course water not far below the surface. The steep bank behind is the former Thames and Severn Canal.

FACILITIES INFORMATION – CRICKLADE TO SOURCE

Refreshments

Cricklade: Cricklade Café, High Street (opposite White Hart); 8am–6pm
(Sat 8am–4pm; Sun 10am–2,30pm).

Cricklade: The White Hart, High Street. Food 12–2.30pm and 7–10pm;
open all day.

Ashton Keynes: The Horse and Jockey, Gosditch Street. 12–3pm and
5.30–11pm; all day weekends.

Ashton Keynes: The White Hart Inn, High Road. Mon 6pm–10pm; Tue–Thu
12pm–2:30pm and 6pm–11pm; Fri 12–2.30pm and 5pm–midnight;
Sat 12pm–3pm and 6pm midnight; Sun 11.30am–10pm.

Somerford Keynes: The Baker's Arms. Food 12–2.45pm and 6–9.45pm;
open all day.

Ewen: The Wild Duck Inn (built in 1563). Real ales. Bar food at lunchtime and
evening. 11am–11pm. (Sun 11–10.30pm).

Kemble: The Tavern Inn (on west side of station). 11.30am–11pm.

Accommodation

Cricklade: The Old Bear, High Street SN6 6AP (01793 75005).

Cricklade: The White Hart Hotel, High Street SN6 6AA (01793 750206,
www.thewhitehartcricklade.co.uk.

Cricklade: The White Lion, High Street SN6 6DA (01793 750999,
www.whitelioncricklade.co.uk).

Waterhay Bridge: Waterhay Farm, Leigh, SN6 6QY (01285 861253).
Cross bridge and turn right.

Ashton Keynes: 1 Cove House SN6 6NS, east of the White Hart (01285 861226).

Ashton Keynes: Wheatleys Farm, High Road SN6 6NX, south of The White Hart
(01285 861310).

Ewen: The Wild Duck Inn GL7 6BY (01285 770310,
www.thewildduckinn.co.uk).

Ewen: Brooklands Farm, GL7 6BU (01285 770487).

Transport

Cricklade: National Rail to Swindon then bus (www.traveline.info;
0871 200 2233).

Source: National Rail from Kemble.

The Source

Tourist Information
Cirencester: The Corinium Museum, Park Street, GL7 2BX (01285 654180).
Swindon: Central Library, Regent Circus, SN1 1QG (01793 530328).

Map
OS Explorer 168 (Stroud) and 169 (Cirencester and Swindon).

APPENDIX A
Optional Prelude: Erith to the Thames Barrier

Where does the Thames Path national trail start? Officially at the Thames Barrier but it is now possible to start further downstream at Erith. From this small former Kentish town on the edge of Greater London there is a continuous 8-mile path to the Barrier. It is a dramatic location with a long pier snaking out into the wide tidal river. This lower extension also offers the opportunity of seeing large working ships on the tidal Thames. But it is remote with no food and few seats until Woolwich.

For those who wish to follow this unofficial prelude to the National Trail, a brief route description is provided below along with a 1:100K route map.

ERITH TO THAMESMEAD

From Erith station, turn right and follow the road through a tunnel. At once go right up a passage. At the far end do not go ahead but turn sharp left up to a road. Cross over and turn right. Go left at the Town Hall. Follow the road past shops and a bus terminus (right). At a junction go left into Erith High Street to find Erith Playhouse.

From the theatre go ahead downhill and just past the old Police Station leave the High Street by turning right to find the river and Erith Causeway. A pilgrim notice is on the left. Follow the promenade with water to the right. Follow the path round the three sides of a dock. At a second dock, part of the naval storehouse site, the path briefly leaves the riverside to go round

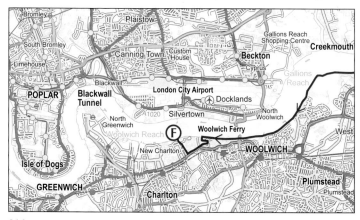

the back of a crane. Round another bend the path rises and the buildings end. Here a path leads inland to Erith Old Church.

Soon the riverside path is under the first of several gantries and conveyors. At one point, the path rises and falls steeply. There is a rare small park with seating.

Just after passing dramatic disused jetties reaching far out into the water, the path is on a stretch known as Jenningtree Point where the Rainham Ferry landed until 1954. There are lorry loading bays inland. Just beyond here, by a Sustrans mile post, is Crabtree Manorway, a long path, leading to woodland at Belvedere.

Soon a huge modern building with a high wide ramp running down to a pier is ahead. This is where waste brought on barges from London is landed for incineration. In earlier times, before separation

and recycling, rubbish was dumped on Rainham and Mucking Marshes. Across the river is Dagenham's Ford works. Having passed through a kissing gate and over a discharge channel, the river view is briefly lost each side of a 'sludge pier' at Halfway Reach. To the left is the sewage works but next door are the Victorian buildings of Crossness Pumping Station.

The river view is restored as the path approaches Thamesmead.

THAMESMEAD TO WOOLWICH ARSENAL

The next landmark is Cross Ness point marked by the red 'lighthouse'. As the path with wild grass gives way to a wide promenade there is the first view ahead of London's tall buildings. The promenade, which continues for some distance, soon crosses the Bexley-Greenwich borough boundary.

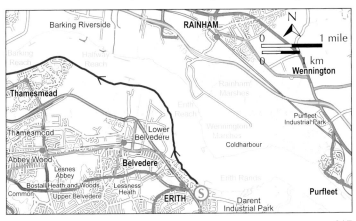

(If you wish to reach bus stops in Thamesmead, at a signpost go up the slope and left along the road.) The promenade narrows to a path after passing Thamesmead Pumping Station on the edge of Thamesmead. Barking Creek flood gateway can be seen opposite. Continue past a drawdock.

On approaching Tripcock Ness, the path joins a higher wide track. Beyond Tripcock Ness 'lighthouse', the river is hidden by trees for some distance. New flats, built on Plumstead Marshes, begin to appear on the left. After some distance the path meets gates and joins a promenade. On turning into a dock do not walk to the upstream side but at once go up a slope and steps to go round the back of a dock. The path continues by the river on the far side. Inland are the original Royal Arsenal buildings. Ahead is Woolwich Arsenal Pier.

WOOLWICH TO THE THAMES BARRIER

(To get to Woolwich Arsenal station, on the far side of Beresford Square, go inland to the main road and gateway.)

Stay by the river beyond the pier. The wide way rises gently to join a promenade where there is a view of the Canary Wharf and City tower blocks. Go round steps by the leisure centre. Where the riverside path ends bear left down to the road which bends left. After a very short distance go right round the Woolwich

Ferry Store (right) to reach the ferry approach road. Cross the road and bear right past a car park to find the riverside path running along the former naval dockyard.

The path runs over several dock entrances between flats and past two riverside gun emplacements (right). The path is up and down steep steps at a viewpoint. (To avoid the steps take the ramp and turn back at the end.). Tate & Lyle is across the river where planes can be seen taking off from London City Airport. The flats on the left are on King Henry's Wharf. (From summer 2017 it should be possible to continue ahead on a ramp taking the path across Trinity Wharf and inland to Warspite Road. Go right into Bowater Road to reach the Thames Barrier.)

Leave the riverside path before the end by going through a gateway where the Thames Path is waymarked (left). Go right at the road junction to follow residential Harlinger Street. Turn left into Ruston Street where there is a view of a tall dockyard chimney. Continue right past a post box. The road curves by a roundabout by McDonald's (left). Cross the end of Warspite Road (right) and pass a former pub to enter Woolwich Road. The dual carriageway runs gently uphill past The White Horse and The Royal Greenwich UTC (right).

The Thames Barrier is reached by going right with the Green Chain Walk which leads to steps at a flood-bank by the Thames Barrier.

APPENDIX B
Further reading

Banks, Leslie and Stanley, Christopher *The Thames: A History from the Air* (Oxford 1990)

Belloc, Hilaire *The Historic Thames: A Portrait of England's Greatest River* (IB Tauris 2008)

Chaplin, Peter H *The Thames from Source to Tideway* (Whittet Books 1982)

Dickens, Charles (jun) *Dictionary of the Thames* (Taurus Press 1972)

Ebel, Suzanne and Impey, Doreen *A Guide to London's Riverside* (Constable 1985)

Elsom, Derek *Taming the Rivers of Oxford* (Oxford Region Thematic Trails, Oxford Polytechnic 1987)

Hatts, Leigh *Country Walks Around London* (David and Charles 1983)

Hatts, Leigh *Pub Walks Along The Thames Path* (Countryside Books 1997)

Hatts, Leigh *Walks Along The Thames Path* (PSL/Haynes 1990)

Hayward, Graham *Stanford's River Thames Companion* (Stanford 1988)

Hibbert, Christopher and Hibbert, Edward *The Encyclopaedia of Oxford* (Papermac 1992)

Jebb, Miles *A Guide to the Thames Path* (Constable 1988)

Jenkins, Alan *The Book of The Thames* (Papermac 1983)

Jerome, Jerome K *Three Men in a Boat* (Penguin Classics (new edition) 2004)

Leapman, Michael *London's River: A History of the Thames* (Pavilion 1991)

Leyland, John *The Thames Illustrated* (British Library, Historical Print Editions 2011)

Livingston, Helen *The Thames Path: Aerofilms Guide* (Ian Allan 1993)

Mackay, Duncan *The Secret Thames* (Ebury 1992)

Pevsner, Nikolaus *The Buildings of England* (Penguin)

Phillips, Geoffrey *Thames Crossings* (David and Charles 1981)

Pritchard, Mari and Carpenter, Humphrey *A Thames Companion* (Oxford 1981)

Rodgers, David *William Morris At Home* (Ebury 1996)

Sharp, David *The Thames Walk* (Ramblers' Association 1990)

Taunt, Henry *A New Map of the River Thames from Oxford to London* (Andesite Press 2015)

Turner, Mark *Pubs of the River Thames* (Prion 2000)

Weightman, Gavin *London's Thames* (John Murray 2004)

Weinreb, Ben and Hibbert, Christopher *The London Encyclopaedia* (Macmillan 2008)

Wilson, DG *The Thames: Record of a Working Waterway* (Batsford 1987)

The Royal River: The Thames from Source to Sea 1885 (Bloomsbury Books 1985)

The Thames Path: Proposed Long Distance Path (Countryside Commission 1989)

Websites

Thames Path (London to Source; companion to this guide with the latest news and updates): www.thamespath.org.uk

Thames Path National Trail official website: www.nationaltrail.co.uk

Old Thames (a growing collection of images old and new from riverside libraries and museums): www.thamespilot.org.uk

LISTING OF CICERONE GUIDES

For full information on all our
guides, books and eBooks, visit
our website:
www.cicerone.co.uk.

Walking – Trekking – Mountaineering – Climbing – Cycling

Over 40 years, Cicerone have built up an outstanding collection of over 300 guides, inspiring all sorts of amazing adventures.

Every guide comes from extensive exploration and research by our expert authors, all with a passion for their subjects. They are frequently praised, endorsed and used by clubs, instructors and outdoor organisations.

All our titles can now be bought as **e-books**, **ePubs** and **Kindle** files and we also have an online magazine – **Cicerone Extra** – with features to help cyclists, climbers, walkers and trekkers choose their next adventure, at home or abroad.

Our website shows any **new information** we've had in since a book was published. Please do let us know if you find anything has changed, so that we can publish the latest details. On our **website** you'll also find great ideas and lots of detailed information about what's inside every guide and you can buy **individual routes** from many of them online.

It's easy to keep in touch with what's going on at Cicerone by getting our monthly **free e-newsletter**, which is full of offers, competitions, up-to-date information and topical articles. You can subscribe on our home page and also follow us on **Facebook** and **Twitter** or dip into our **blog**.

Cicerone – the very best guides for exploring the world.

CICERONE

2 Police Square Milnthorpe Cumbria LA7 7PY
Tel: 015395 62069 info@cicerone.co.uk
www.cicerone.co.uk and **www.cicerone-extra.com**